AMERICA
Adventures in Eyewitness History

AMERICA

Adventures in Eyewitness History

RHODA HOFF

New York   HENRY Z. WALCK, Inc.   1962

LIBRARY OF CONGRESS CATALOG CARD NUMBER: 62-17843
PRINTED IN THE UNITED STATES OF AMERICA

Acknowledgments

Grateful acknowledgment is made to the publishers who kindly gave permission to adapt and use the following material:

"The Discovery of the Mississippi," from *The Jesuit Relations and Allied Comments: Travels and Explorations of the Jesuit Missionaries in North America (1610–1791)*, edited by Edna Kenton. Albert & Charles Boni, Inc., 1925.

"Braddock's Defeat," from *Journal of Captain Robert Cholmley's Batman*, edited by Charles Hamilton. University of Oklahoma Press, 1960.

"A Snow Storm in the Country," from *Sketches of Eighteenth Century America*, by St. John de Crèvecoeur. Yale University Press, 1925.

"General George Washington," reprinted by permission of Dodd, Mead & Company from *Our Revolutionary Forefathers*, by Marquis de Marbois.

"A Letter from New York," from *Letters from America, 1776–1779*, translated by Ray W. Pettingill. The Riverside Press, Houghton Mifflin Co., 1924.

"The Surrender at Yorktown," from *The Revolutionary Journal of Baron Ludwig von Closen,* translated by Evelyn M. Acomb. University of North Carolina Press, 1958.

"Thomas Jefferson," from *Jeffersonian America,* by Sir Augustus John Foster. Henry E. Huntington Library and Art Gallery, 1954.

"The Pioneer," from *Journey to America,* by Alexis de Tocqueville. Yale University Press, 1960.

"A Frontier Trading Post," from *Journal of Rudolph Friederich Kurz,* edited by J. N. B. Dewitt. Translated by Myrtis Jarell. Bureau of American Ethnology, The Smithsonian Institution.

"Summer on the Prairie," from *Portrait of America: Letters of Henryk Sienkiewicz,* translated by Charles Morley. Columbia University Press, 1959.

"The Promised Land," from the book by Mary Antin. Houghton Mifflin Co., 1912.

Contents

THE NEW WORLD

GROWTH OF A NEW NATION

Preface

THE DICTIONARY TELLS US that history is "a narrative of events."
But this terse statement is a somewhat over-simplified definition.
For it makes no distinction between what I should like to call
History with a capital *H* and history with a small *h*. By History
with a capital *H*, I mean History seen in the perspective with
which only time can endow it. This is the history of the scholar.
Sitting in his study long after the event he describes has taken
place, he is in a position to view it objectively, to set it in a
frame of "before" and "after" and to filter out of his historical
brew the exaggerations and inconsistencies that have seeped
into it by way of the human ego and the human emotions.

History with a small *h*, on the other hand, is history as it is
recalled by a person who reports on something he himself has
seen or heard or experienced. This is an undigested kind of
history, a message from the heat of the battle. It wraps a fact in
the "blood, sweat and tears" of a living, breathing man or
woman—any man or woman. This is an exciting and flavorful
approach but it must by its very nature be something of an
adventure, subject to the same risks and rewards that physical
adventure brings. For history seen through one pair of eyes is

not history in the round. What it gains in intimacy, it loses in focus and perspective. But once we are aware of the fact that we are dealing only with one person's truth, we are forewarned and forearmed. Then we can enjoy a contact with the past that is extraordinarily vivid, amazingly alive.

The reports which make up this book have been selected, like points in a graph, to plot the curve of American history beginning with a December day in 1620 when a company of brave and dedicated English men and women landed on the shore of a cold New World ready to pay with their lives, if they must, for the right to worship their God as they liked and to live in freedom. The book ends with a day almost three hundred years later when a little Jewish girl arrived from Russia for much the same reasons. The fact that she found, instead of a wilderness, a great and thriving country, a country she called "The Promised Land," is the triumph of the American story.

None of the men and women in this book are Americans by birth. They are settlers, soldiers, journalists and quite ordinary tourists. What they have to say is sometimes complimentary and sometimes critical. In the belief that it is stimulating as well as salutary to see ourselves as others see us, all the witnesses have been allowed to testify with a minimum of editorial interference.

Occasionally spelling has been modernized in the interest of readability and, when space was at a premium, cuts have been made. For there were hundreds of years to cover, and so many witnesses to be heard that in order to give representation to many different facets of American life some of the reports had to be pruned. But in no case was an idea distorted or a meaning altered. There has been no tampering with the intention of the witness. And if at times an excerpt is shorter than the span of the reader's interest, perhaps it will act as an invitation to him to go back to the original source and explore there at greater length the writer who in this book can only be sampled.

Finally, it is the hope—and the belief—of the editor that these personal stories will project a living picture of a time, a place or a person, an eyewitness picture, subject, of course, to the risks and the rewards that are the price and the profit of all adventure.

R. H.

AMERICA
Adventures in Eyewitness History

THE NEW WORLD

1620

THE FIRST LANDING AT PLYMOUTH
by Governor William Bradford

ON SEPTEMBER 16TH, 1620, a group of 102 men, women and children, among them William Bradford, sailed from Plymouth, England, in a ship called the *Mayflower,* to plant a colony in the New World. Because this company was willing to travel to the ends of the earth for the sake of their religious beliefs, people called them the Pilgrims. Persecuted in England for their faith, they had first emigrated to Holland; but after living there for eleven years their children had begun to forget they were English. So the Pilgrims decided to go on a new pilgrimage, this time to a country that was still wild and largely uninhabited; a brand new country where they would be free to worship in accordance with their faith and yet, as English colonists, keep their identity as Englishmen.

The *Mayflower* landed on the Massachusetts coast on the 11th of December, 1620. That first winter was a desperate one; half the group died of cold and scurvy. But the Pilgrims were a resolute, hard-working group, and their leaders were strong and resourceful men. When spring came the survivors planted crops, built themselves permanent homes—and wrote to their parent company for re-enforcements. That fall a second ship arrived from England. It brought supplies of all kinds and new settlers to take the place of those who had died.

Bradford was one of the leaders of the young colony. Born in Yorkshire, England, the son of well-to-do parents, he had been one of the first to go to Holland, where he had supported himself as a silk-weaver. In 1621, when John Carver, the first governor of Plymouth Colony, died, William Bradford was elected to succeed him. Except for five years, he held the office of governor until his death in 1657. A man of wise and dauntless character, he guided Plymouth Colony during its critical early years and led it to prosperity and success.

After long beating at sea, they fell with that land which is called Cape Cod. After some deliberation had amongst themselves, and with the master of the ship, they tacked about, and resolved to stand for the southward (the wind and weather being fair) to find some place, about Hudson's river for their habitation. But after they had sailed the course about half the day, they fell amongst dangerous shoals and roaring breakers, and they were so far entangled therewith, as they conceived themselves in great danger and the wind shrinking upon them withall, they resolved to bear up again for the cape; and thought themselves happy to get out of those dangers, before night overtook them, as by God's good provision they did. And the next day they got into the cape harbor where they rode in safety.

Being thus arrived in a good harbor, and brought safe to land, they fell upon their knees and blessed the God of heaven, who had brought them over the vast and furious ocean and delivered them from all the perils and miseries thereof again to set their feet on the firm and stable earth, their proper element. Being thus passed the vast ocean and a sea of troubles before in their preparation, they had now no friends to welcome them, no inns to entertain, or refresh their weatherbeaten bodies, no houses, or much less towns to repair to, to seek for succor. It is recorded in scripture as a mercy to the apostle and his ship-wrecked company, that the barbarians showed them no small kindness in refreshing them, but these savage barbarians, when they met with them (as will appear) were readier to

4

fill their sides full of arrows than otherwise. And for the season it was winter, and they that know the winters of that country, know them to be sharp and violent, and subject to cruel and fierce storms, dangerous to travel to known places, much more to search an unknown coast.

Besides what could they see, but a hideous and desolate wilderness, full of wild beasts and wild men, and what multitudes there might be of them they knew not; neither could they (as it were) go up to the top of pisgah, to view from this wilderness, a more goodly country to feed their hopes; for which way so ever they turned their eyes (save upward to the heavens) they could have little solace or content, in respect of any outward objects, for summer being done, all things stand upon them with a weather-beaten face; and the whole country (full of woods and thickets) represented a wild and savage hew. If they looked behind them, there was the mighty ocean which they had passed, and was now as a main bar, and gulf, to separate them from all the civilised parts of the world. If it be said they had a ship to succor them, it is true; but what heard they daily from the master and company? but that with speed they should look out a place (with their shallop) where they would be, at some near distance; for the season was such, as he would not stir from thence, till a safe harbor was discovered by them, where they would be, and he might go without danger; and that victuals consumed apace, but he must and would keep sufficient for themselves and their return; yet it was muttered by some, that if they got not a place in time, they would turn them and their goods ashore and leave them.

What could now sustain them but the spirit of God and his grace? May not and ought not the children of these fathers rightly say, our fathers were *English men which came over this great ocean, and were ready to perish in this wilderness, but they cried unto the Lord, and he heard their voice, and looked on their adversity. Let them therefore praise the Lord, because he is good; and his mercies*

5

endure forever. Yea, let them which have been redeemed of the Lord, show how he hath delivered them from the hand of the oppressor. When they wandered in the desert wilderness out of the way, and found no city to dwell in, both hungry and thirsty, their soul was overwhelmed in them. Let them confess before the Lord his loving kindness, and his wonderful works before the sons of men.

1621

A TREATY OF PEACE WITH THE INDIANS
From the Journal of Governors William Bradford and Edward Winslow

ONE OF THE MOST DIFFICULT problems the colonists faced after they reached America was how to treat with the Indians who were their neighbors. The English government had not yet formulated an Indian policy so that it was up to each company of settlers to deal with the Indians as they thought best.

The Pilgrims decided to make a treaty of peace with Chief Massasoit, and it is to the credit of both the Indians and the settlers that both sides were faithful to their contract as long as Massasoit lived. After his death, however, a new chief betrayed the treaty, and in 1675 the era of peaceful relations between the Pilgrims and the settlers came to an end.

Thursday, the 22nd of March [1621] was a very fair, warm day. About noon Samoset came again and Squanto and signified unto us, that their great sagamore, Masasoyt, was hard by, with Quadequina, his brother, and all their men. After an hour the king came to the top of a hill over against us, and had in his train sixty men, that we could well behold them, and they us. We were not willing to send our governor to them, and they were unwilling to come to us. So Squanto went again unto him, who brought word that we should send one to parley with him, which we did, which was Edward Winslow, to know his mind and to signify the mind and will of our governor, which was to have trading and peace with him. We sent to the king a pair of knifes, and a copper chain with a jewel on it. To Quadequina we sent likewise a knife, and a jewel to hang in his ear, and withal a pot of strong water, a good quantity of biscuit, and some butter; which was all willingly accepted.

Our messenger made a speech unto him, that King James saluted him with words of love and peace, and did accept him as his friend and ally; and that our governor desired to see him and to truck with him, and to confirm a peace with him, as his next neighbor. After he had eaten and drunk himself, and given the rest to his company, he looked upon our messenger's sword and armor, with intimation of his desire to buy it; but, on the other side, our messenger showed his unwillingness to part with it. In the end, he left him in the custody of Quadequina, his brother, and came over the brook, and some twenty men following him, leaving all their bows and arrows behind them. We kept six or seven hostages for our messenger. Captain Standish and Master Williamson met the king at the brook, with half a dozen musketeers. They saluted him, and he them; so, one going over, the one on the one side, and the other on the other, conducted him to a house then in building, where he placed a green rug and three or four cushions. Then instantly came our governor, with drum and trumpet after him, and some few musketeers. After salutations, our governor kissing his hands, the king kissed him; and so they sat down. The governor called for some strong water, and drunk to him; and he drunk a great draught, that made him sweat all the while after. He called for a little fresh meat, which the king did eat willingly, and did give his followers. Then they treated of peace, which was:

7

1. That neither he nor any of his should injure or do hurt to any of our people.

2. And if any of his did hurt any of ours, he should send the offender, that we might punish him.

3. That if any of our tools were taken away, when our people were at work, he should cause them to be restored; and if ours did any harm to any of his, we should do the like to them.

4. If any did unjustly war against him, we would aid him; if any did war against us, he should aid us.

5. He should send to his neighbor confederates to certify them of this, that they might not wrong us, but might be likewise comprised in the conditions of peace.

6. That when their men came to us, they should leave their bows and arrows behind them, as we should do our pieces when we came to them.

Lastly, that doing thus, King James would esteem of him as friend and ally.

1636

THE INDIAN WARS IN NEW ENGLAND
by William Hubbard, A.M.

"There was a nation of the Indians in the southern parts of New England called Pequods," writes the Reverend Hubbard, minister of Ipswich, "seated in a fair navigable river, twelve miles to the eastward of the mouth of the great and famous river of Connecticut; who, being a more fierce, cruel and war-like people than the rest of the Indians, came down out of the more inland parts of the continent, and by force seized upon one of the goodliest places near the sea, and became a terror to all their neighbors [and] being flushed with victories over their fellow-Indians, they began to thirst after the blood of any foreigners, English or Dutch that accidentally came amongst them, in a way of trade, or upon other accounts." This judgment is probably true enough, but, on reading the account that follows, it must be evident to any fair-minded observer that the fault for bad Indian-colonist relations cannot be laid entirely at the door of the "savages." In any case a fierce war broke out between the Pequots and the colonists in 1637. The white men won, and the Pequot tribe was practically destroyed.

Amongst the soldiers that were sent under Capt. Endicot, were twenty that belonged to Saybrook-fort, and were appointed to stay there, to defend the place against the Pequods: After the said Capt. and the rest were departed, those twenty lay wind-bound in the Pequod harbor, and the meanwhile went all of them ashore, with sacks to fetch some of the Pequod's corn; and having fetched each man one sackful to their boat, they returned for more, and having loaded themselves, the Indians set upon them, so they laid down their corn, and gave fire upon the Indians, and the Indians shot their arrows against them; the place was open about the distance of a musket shot; the Indians kept the covert, save when they came forth at a time and discharged their arrows: the English put themselves in a single file, and ten only that had pieces that could reach them, shot, the others stood ready to keep them from breaking in. So they continued most part of the afternoon; the English, as they supposed, killed divers of them, and hurt others; and the Indians wounded but one of the English, who was armed, all the rest being without: For they shot their arrows compass-wise, so as they could easily see and avoid them standing single, then always gathered up their arrows: At the last, the Indians being weary of the sport, gave the English leave to retire to their boat. This was in October, 1636.

About two days after, five men of Saybrook went up the river about four miles to fetch hay out of a meadow on the Pequod side: The grass was so high as some Pequods hiding themselves in it, set upon the English before they were aware, and took one that had hay on his back, the rest fled to their boat, one of them had five arrows in him, yet recovered: He that was taken was a goodly young man, whose name was Butterfield; whereupon the meadow was ever afterward called Butterfield meadow.

Two Indians assaulted the house of one Tozer, at Newechewannuck, wherein were fifteen persons, yet all women and children, who without doubt had all of them fallen into the merciless hands of the two cruel and barbarous caitiffs, had not a young maid of about 18 years of age, first espied them, who being endowed with more courage than ordinarily the rest of the sex use to be, first shut to the door, whereby they were denied entrance till the rest within escaped to the next house that was better fortified; that young heroess kept the door fast against them so long, till the Indians had chopped it into pieces with their hatchets, when entering the house they knocked the poor maid down with their hatchets, and gave her many wounds, leaving her for dead upon the place; after which they passed on toward the next dwelling, on their way meeting with two children that had escaped the house first broken open by them, they killed one of them, of three years old, which could not follow fast enough and carried away the other of seven years old, which was returned safe within half a year after. The poor maid that had ventured her life so far to save many others, was by a strange Providence enabled to recover so much strength after they were gone, as to repair to the next garrison, where she was soon after healed of her wounds and restored to perfect health.

1673

THE DISCOVERY OF THE MISSISSIPPI
From the Journal of Father Jacques Marquette

FROM THE BEGINNING of her colonization adventure in North America, France made a serious effort to convert the Indians to Christianity. Devoted missionaries accompanied French soldiers and explorers into the wilderness, staying behind after the conquerors left, to live and work among the Indians. One of these French missionary-priests was Father Jacques Marquette (1637–1675), a member of the Society of Jesus.

Indian tribes who lived near the Great Lakes had told the Count de Frontenac, Governor of New France, about a mighty river called the Mississippi. In 1672 the governor asked Father Marquette, who had great influence with the Indians and knew many of their languages, to join Louis Joliet on a trip to that river.

The two men left St. Ignace, Michigan, in the spring of 1673. Their route lay through Lake Michigan, Green Bay and the Fox River. Carrying their canoes over a long portage, they arrived at the Wisconsin and followed it to its meeting with the Mississippi, which they entered on June 15th. The two explorers floated downstream until they approached Spanish territory, when, fearing they might be taken captive, they decided to turn back.

Father Marquette and Louis Joliet returned safely from their difficult five-month journey, but two years later, while on a trip to found a new mission among the Indians of Illinois, Father Marquette fell ill. He died on May 18th, 1675, near what is now the site of Ludington, Michigan.

We safely entered Mississippi on the 17th of June, with a Joy that I cannot express.

We gently followed its Course, which runs toward the south and southeast, as far as the 42nd degree Latitude. We saw only deer and cattle, bustards and Swans without wings, because they drop Their plumage in This country. From time to time, we came upon mon-

11

strous fish, one of which struck our Canoe with such violence that I Thought that it was a great tree, about to break the Canoe to pieces. On another occasion, we saw on The water a monster with the head of a tiger, a sharp nose Like That of a wildcat, with whiskers and straight, Erect ears; the head was grey and the Neck quite black; but We saw no more creatures of this sort.

We continued to advance, but, As we knew not whither we were going, we kept well on guard. On this account, we make only a small fire on land, toward evening, to cook our meals; and, after supper, we remove Ourselves as far from it as possible, and pass the night in our Canoes, which we anchor in the river at some distance from the shore.

Finally on the 25th of June, we perceived at the water's edge some tracks of men, and a narrow and somewhat beaten path leading to a fine prairie. We resolved to go and reconnoitre it. We silently followed The narrow path, and, after walking about 2 leagues, We discovered a village on the bank of a river, and two others on a Hill distant about half a league from the first. We Decided that it was time to reveal ourselves. This we did by Shouting with all Our energy, and stopped, without advancing any further. On hearing the shout, the savages quickly issued from their Cabins, And having probably recognized us as frenchmen, especially when they saw a black gown, they deputed four old men to come and speak to us. They walked slowly, and raised their pipes toward the sun, seemingly offering them to it to smoke—without, however, saying a word. I spoke with them first, and asked them who they were. They replied that they were Illinois; and, as a token of peace, they offered us their pipes to smoke. They afterward invited us to enter their Village, where all the people impatiently awaited us.

When we reached the Village of the great Captain, We saw him in the entrance of his Cabin, between two old men,—all three erect and naked, and holding their Calumet turned toward the sun. He afterward offered us his Calumet, and made us smoke while we entered his Cabin, where we received all their usual kind Attentions.

Seeing all assembled and silent, I spoke to them. When I had finished my speech, the Captain arose, and resting His hand upon the head of a little Slave whom he wished to give us, he spoke thus: "I thank thee, Black Gown, and thee, O frenchman, for having taken so much trouble to come to visit us. Never has the earth been so beautiful, or the sun so Bright as to-day; Never has our river been so Calm, or so clear of Rocks, which your canoes have Removed in passing; never has our tobacco tasted so good, or our corn appeared so fine, as We now see Them. Here is my son, whom I give thee to Show thee my Heart. I beg thee to have pity on me, and all my Nation. It is thou who Knowest the great Spirit who has made us all. Beg him to give me life and health, and to come and dwell with us, in order to make us Know him." Having said this, he placed the little Slave near us, and gave us a second present, consisting of an altogether mysterious Calumet, upon which they place more value than upon a Slave and, by a third, he begged us on behalf of all his Nation not to go farther, on account of the great dangers to which we Exposed ourselves.

I replied that I Feared not death, and that I regarded no happiness greater than that of losing my life for the glory of Him who has made all. This is what these poor people cannot Understand.

The Council was followed by a great feast. The first course was a great wooden platter full of sagamité,—that is to say, meal of Indian corn boiled in water, and seasoned with fat. The Master of Ceremonies filled a spoon with sagamité three or four times, and put it to my mouth As if I were a little Child. He did The same to Monsieur Jollyet. As a second course, he caused a second platter to be brought, on which were three fish. He took some pieces of them, removed the bones therefrom, and after blowing on them to cool Them he put them in our mouths As one would give food to a bird. For the third course, they brought a large dog, that had just been killed; but, when they learned that we did not eat this meat, they removed it from before us. Finally, the 4th course was a piece of wild ox, The fattest morsels of which were placed in our mouths.

Father Marquette and Monsieur Joliet pursued their exploration of the Mississippi until they were at a latitude of 33 degrees 40 minutes. Here they met some Indians who advised them to go no further as they would expose themselves to a very warlike tribe of Indians, allied to the Spaniards, who would threaten them with great danger.

Monsieur Jollyet and I held another Council, to deliberate upon what we should do—whether we should push on, or remain content with the discovery which we had made. After extensively considering that we were not far from the gulf of Mexico, and that, beyond a doubt, the Mississippi river discharges into the florida or Mexican gulf, and not to The east in Virginia, or to the west in California, because in that case our route would have been to The west, or the south-west, whereas we had always continued It toward the south. We further considered that we exposed ourselves to the risk of losing the results of this voyage, of which we could give no information if we proceeded to fling ourselves into the hands of the Spaniards, who, without doubt, would at least have detained us all captives. Finally, we had obtained all the information that could be desired in regard to this discovery. All these reasons induced us to decide upon Returning.

A JOURNEY WITH THE INDIANS THROUGH THE ILLINOIS PRAIRIES
by Father Gabriel Marest

FATHER GABRIEL MAREST, like Father Marquette, was a member of the Society of Jesus who had come to America to do missionary work among the Indians. Stationed at Cascaskias, a village on the Illinois prairies, he set out on the Friday of Passion Week to meet with his superior at a village called Michillimacinac. His plan was to stop off on the way at a village of the Peouaria Indians where a missionary father had recently died, in order to see if it would be wise to send another member of the Society of Jesus to take charge of the vacant mission. Father Marest was accompanied on his journey by two members of the Peouaria tribe.

Journeys which are made in this country should not be compared with those in Europe. There you find from time to time villages and towns, and houses in which you can rest, bridges or boats to cross the rivers, beaten paths which lead to your destination, and persons who can place you in the right way, if you have strayed. Here there is nothing of the kind, and we travelled for twelve days without meeting a single soul. At one time we found ourselves on prairies which were boundless to our view, cut up by brooks and rivers, but without discovering any path which could guide us, and then again it became necessary to open a passage through dense forests, in the midst of brushwood covered with thorns and briars, and at other times we had to cross marshes filled with mire, in which we sometimes sank to the waist.

After having been excessively fatigued during the day, we were obliged to take our repose at night on the grass or on some branches, exposed to the wind, to the rain, and to the injurious effects of the atmosphere. We were happy indeed if we found ourselves near some stream, but if not, no matter how dry we were, the night passed without our being able to alleviate our thirst. We kindled a fire, and when we had killed any game on our way, we roasted pieces of it, which we eat with some ears of Indian corn, if we had any of them.

Besides these inconveniences, common to all those who travel through these deserted lands, we had the addition also of hunger during the whole of our journey. It was not because we did not see great numbers of stags and deer, and particularly of buffaloes, but our Indians were not able to kill any. A rumor they had heard the day before our departure that the country was infested by parties of the enemy prevented them from carrying their guns, for fear of being discovered by the report when they fired. Thus, they could use nothing but their arrows, and the buffaloes which they hit, fled, carrying with them the arrows by which they had been pierced, and went to die in some distant place.

In all other things these poor people took great care of me. They carried me on their shoulders when it was necessary to cross any stream, and when we came to deep rivers, they collected many pieces of dry wood which they tied together, and making me seat myself on this kind of boat, they transported themselves by swimming, and pushed me before them to the other side.

It was not without reason that they feared meeting with any war party of the enemy, for they would have received no quarter from them. Either their heads would have been cut off, or at best they would have been made prisoners, to be burnt at last before a slow fire, or to be used for food in their feasts. Nothing can be more frightening than these wars of our Indians. They are commonly found in parties of twenty, or thirty, or forty men. Sometimes these parties consist only of six or seven persons, and in this case they are the most formidable. Their method is to follow on the trail of their enemies, and to kill each one when he is sleeping, or what is better, to place themselves in ambush in the neighborhood of a village, to cut off the head of the first who comes out, and to carry off his scalp to make of it a trophy among his countrymen.

As soon as one of these braves has killed his enemy, he draws his knife, and cuts round the head, taking off the skin with the hair, which he carries in triumph to his village. At times they content themselves with making prisoners. The fate of these prisoners is very sad, for often they burn them at a slow fire, and, at other times, cook them in their kettles to make a feast for all their warriors.

During the first day of our departure we found some traces of a party of these warriors. I could not but admire the sharp-sightedness of our Indians. They showed me their tracks on the grass, distinguished where they had set down, where they had walked, and what was their number. It was a happy circumstance for me that a panic did not seize them at this moment, as they would have left me entirely alone in the midst of the woods. But a little while afterwards, I myself, gave them a terrible fright. A swelling which I had in the feet made me walk slowly, and they had got a very little in advance of me, without my having paid any attention to it. I suddenly perceived that I was alone and immediately began to call them, but they did not make me any answer, not doubting but that I had fallen in with a party of warriors. I redoubled my cries and their fear augmented more and more. The two Indians who were idolators now began to take to flight, but the catachumen, drew a little nearer to see what was the matter. When he had perceived that there was nothing to fear, he made a sign to his comrades: then, approaching me, he said in a trembling voice, "You have given us a great fright, but as for me, I was resolved to die with you, rather than abandon you."

At the beginning of the journey I had made some blisters which I neglected. As the fear of meeting with parties of the enemy made us take long journeys and we passed the night in the midst of brushwood and thickets so that no foe could approach us without being heard; as at other times we did not dare to light a fire for fear of being discovered, the fatigues we were obliged to undergo reduced me to a sad state. I could not walk except upon those sores, which so touched the Indians, who accompanied me, that they formed the resolution of carrying me by turns. This service they rendered me during the two following days, but having reached the Illinois river, and not being more than twenty-five leagues from the *Peouarias,* I engaged one of my Indians to go on before, to give notice to the French of my arrival.

On the third day, I saw a number of my French arrive at noon who brought me a canoe and some refreshments. They embarked me in their canoe, and as I had not the least inconvenience to suffer, the repose and good treatment I enjoyed, very soon reestablished me. It was, however, more than ten days before I was able to bear my weight upon my feet.

1733

THE ESTABLISHMENT OF THE COLONY OF GEORGIA
by an Anonymous Eyewitness

JAMES OGLETHORPE, the founder and first governor of the colony of Georgia was first a general in the British army and then a member of Parliament. His reasons for wanting to found a colony in the New World reflected both of these earlier activities. As a soldier he knew that England needed a buffer state at the southern end of her American colonial holdings to protect her against aggression by the Spaniards who were settled in nearby Florida; as a member of Parliament he knew that there were many debtors in English prisons who were deserving of a second chance and an opportunity to begin life anew. With the help of some other public-spirited Englishmen, he obtained a grant of land between the Savannah and the Altamaha rivers.

In 1732 General Oglethorpe sailed from England with 116 carefully selected colonists. They arrived in Charlestown on January 13th, 1733, and set to work almost immediately building their first settlement near what is now Savannah.

Georgia was the last colony to be planted in the New World and it realized the twofold aims of its founder. The Spaniards did attack as Oglethorpe had prophesied, and he defeated them so decisively that they retreated to Florida and never came back again. And in the course of the years Georgia became a refuge for debtors and the oppressed of Europe.

Charlestown, Jan. 20 (1733). On Saturday night, January 13, 1733, came to anchor off our bar, a ship with about 120 people for settling the new colony of Georgia, in which was James Oglethorpe, Esq. who came ashore that night and was extremely well received by his excellency, our governor. The next morning he went aboard and the ship sailed for Port Royal and, we hear, there are two more ships with people (which will make the number five hundred), expected daily.

While the colony refreshed themselves, Mr. Oglethorpe went up the river and chose a situation for a town, and entered into a treaty with Tomo-Chi-Chi, the micco, or chief of the only nation of Indians living in it. He returned on the twenty-fourth day, and they celebrated the Sunday following as a day of Thanksgiving for their safe arrival.

On the thirtieth the colony embarked on board a sloop of seventy tons and five periaugers, and made sail, but were forced by a storm to put in at a place called the look-out, and to lie there all night. The next day they arrived at John's, where they found huts capable to contain them all, and a plentiful supper of venison. They embarked the next day, and in the afternoon arrived at the place intended for the town.

Being arrived on the first of February, at the intended town before night, they erected four large tents, sufficient to hold all the people, being one for each tything; they landed their bedding and other little necessaries, and all the people lay on shore. The ground they encamped upon is the edge of the river where the key is intended to be.

Until the seventh was spent in making a crane and unloading the goods; which done, Mr. Oglethorpe divided the people, employing part in clearing the land for seed, part in beginning the palisade, and the remainder in felling the trees where the town is to stand.

Colonel Bell arrived with a message from the general assembly for Mr. Oglethorpe and a letter from his excellency, Governor Johnson. Colonel Bull brought with him four negroes, who were sawyers, to assist the colony, and also brought provision for them, being resolved to put the trust to no expense, and by this means to bestow his benefaction in the most noble and useful manner.

On the ninth day, Mr. Oglethorpe and Colonel Bull marked out the square, the streets and forty lots for houses for the town, and the first house (which was ordered to be made of clapboards) was begun that day.

The town lies on the south side of the river Savannah, upon a flat on the top of a hill, and sixty yards of it is reserved between it and the key. The river washes the foot of the hill, which stretches along the side of it about a mile and forms a terrace forty feet perpendicular above high water.

1755

BRADDOCK'S DEFEAT
From the Journal of Captain Robert Cholmley's Batman

As THE BRITISH AND FRENCH colonies grew stronger and more numerous, friction developed inevitably between the rival powers. After a long period of minor disputes, war finally broke out in 1754.

The first battle was fought near the site of what is now Pittsburgh. Led by General Edward Braddock and guided by a young American colonist, Captain George Washington, 1300 British soldiers were ambushed in a forest near the Monongahela River by a much smaller force of French and Indians. The British soldiers, in their red uniforms that were more suitable to a parade ground than to wilderness fighting, lined up in classic battle formation. They offered an easy target to the French and Indians who fought Indian-style, breaking ranks and shooting from behind trees. The veteran British regulars stood their ground for three hours, then broke rank and fled.

But victory in this battle did not do the French any lasting good, for in the end they lost the war. And in 1763, by the Treaty of Paris, France was forced to cede to Great Britain all her American holdings with the exception of two small islands off the coast of Newfoundland.

Wednesday July the 9th. The Advance Party Marched at two in the Morning, Consisting of two grannadier Companies and a hundred Pattallion. My Master Commanded the Pattallion. We marched to take Possession of a Pass Over the River which is called Muningahele River, we having all the morning two pieces of Cannon which was very troublesome to get forward before any Road was Cut which there was not at that time for the working party being behind at that time. A Bout Eight in the Morning we Came to the River after Marching Near Seven Miles. When we Came Close to the River some of our men said they saw great many of the French Indiens on the Other side of the River. Some said there was not Any but to be shure Colonel Gage who Commanded the Party Ordered the Cannon to be taken off the Carriges and to be drawn Over by the men, Ready to Ingage if accation. The men all marched Over in line of Battle with the Cannon till they came to the Other side of the River where we had a Bank to Rise Eight yards perpendquler that we was Obliged to Sloape before we Could Rise the hill. The River is betwixt two and three hundred yards over and not much more than knee deep. After we had Rose the Bank we had not a Bove two hundred yards to Frayzor's Plantation [The cabin of John Fraser, a Scottish trader, had recently been burned by the Indians, and Braddock's soldiers found only its charred remains.] where we marched and our Command went no further at that time. So as soon as we arrived their, the Sentryes was posted and everything made secure. The men that had anything to Eate they Eate it for their Brechfast, it being then about half an hour after Nine, but I believe where there was one that had anything to Eate their was twenty that had Nothing. Some men had Nothing most of the day Before. My Master Eat a little Ham that I had and a Bit of gloster Shire Cheese and I milked the Cow and made him a little milk Punch which he drank a little. About half an hour after ten the working party Came Over the River and about at Eleven the grand Army begins to Come Over. As soon as they Came to the River we Rec'd Orders to march on again. Sir John Sincklare asked Colonel Gage if he would take the two piece of cannon with us again. Colonel Gage Answered, no Sir I think not, for I do not think we Shall have much Occation for them and they being troubolsome to get forwards before the Roads are Cut. So we began our March again, Beating the Grannadiers March all the way, Never seasing. There Never was an Army in the Worlds in more Spirits than we where, thinking of Reaching Fort de Cain the day following as we was then only five miles from it. But we had not got above a mile and a half before three of our guides in the froont of me above ten yards spyed

22

the Indiens lay'd down before us. He Immediately discharged his piece, turned Round his horse Cried, the Indiens was upon us. My Master Called me to give me his horse which I tooke from him and the Ingagement began. Immediately they began to Ingage us in a Half Moon and still Continued Surrounding us more and more. Before the whole of the Army got up we had about two thirds of our men Cut off that Ingaged at the First. My Master died before we was ten Minuits Ingaged. They Continually made us retreat, they haveing always a large marke to shoute at and we having only to shoute at them behind trees or laid on their Bellies. We was drawn up in large Bodies together, a ready mark. They need not have taken sight at us for they Always had a large Mark, but if we saw of them five or six at one time was a great sight and they Either on their Bellies or Behind trees or Runingfrom one tree to another almost by the ground. The genll had five horses Shot under him. He always strove to keep the men together but I believe their might be two hundred of the American Soldiers that fought behind Trees and I believe they did the most Execution of Any. Our Indiens behaved very well for the Small Quantity of them. They began to Inclose us more and more till they Had Nigh Inclosed us in. If it was not for their Barbaras usage which we knew they would treat us, we should Never have fought them as long as we did, but having only death before us made the men fight Almost longer than they was able. I Expected nothing but Death for Every Oone of us, for they had us surrounded all but a little in the rear, which they strove for with all their Force. But our men knowing the Conciquance of it preserved the pass till we Retreated. The generall was wounded and a great many Officers was killed with about five hundred private men, and about four hundred wounded out of Better than twelve hundred. The Ingagement began before One and Ended half an hour after four, when we Retreated.

23

1760

NEW YORK CITY AND KING'S COLLEGE
by Andrew Burnaby

THE REVEREND ANDREW BURNABY, Vicar of Greenwich, England, made a trip through the American colonies in the years 1759 and 1760. Burnaby came to America with an open mind and the notes he made on the spot were, as he says, the "fruit of the most impartial inquiries and best intelligence that I was able to procure."

Intelligent, observant and fair-minded, he tried always to see both sides of a problem. An example of this balanced approach is shown in his assessment of the difficulties between the mother country and her colonies: "Let every Englishman and American," he writes, "but for a moment substitute themselves in each other's place, and, I think a mode of reconciliation will soon take effect.— Every American will then perceive the reasonableness of acknowledging the supremacy of the British legislature; and every Englishman perhaps the hardship of being taxed where there is no representation in assent." Burnaby took a lively interest in education, and the new King's College, now Columbia University, in New York City, drew his careful attention.

On his return to England, Burnaby assembled the notes he had taken into a book which because of its accuracy and impartiality is still one of the best sources of information on colonial America.

This city is situated upon the point of a small island, lying open to the bay on one side, and on the other included between the North and East rivers and commands a fine prospect of water, the Jerseys, Long Island, Staten Island, and several others, which lie scattered in the bay. It contains between 2 and 3,000 houses, and 16 or 17,000 inhabitants, is tolerably well built, and has several good houses. The streets are paved and very clean but in general they are narrow; there are two or three, indeed, which are spacious and airy, particularly the Broad Way. The houses in this street have most of them a row of trees before them; which form an agreeable shade, and produce a pretty effect. The whole length of the town is something more than a mile; the breadth of it about half an one. The situation is, I believe, healthy; but it is subject to one great inconvenience, which is the want of fresh water; so that the inhabitants are obliged to have it brought from springs at some distance out of town. There are several public buildings, though but few that deserve attention. The college, when finished, will be exceedingly handsome; it is to be built on three sides of a quadrangle, fronting Hudson's or North River, and will be the most beautifully situated of any college, I believe, in the world. At present only one wing is finished, which is of stone, and consists of twenty-four apartments; each having a large sitting room, with a study, and bed chamber. They are obliged to make use of some of these apartments for a master's lodge, library, chapel, hall, etc. but as soon as the whole shall be completed, there will be proper apartments for each of these offices. The name of it is King's College.

Art and sciences have made no greater progress here than in the other colonies; but as a subscription library has been lately opened, and every one seems zealous to promote learning, it may be hoped that they will hereafter advance faster than hitherto. The college is established upon the same plan as that in the Jerseys, except that this at New York professes the principles of the Church of England. At present the state of it is far from being flourishing or so good as might be wished. Its fund does not exceed 10,000£ currency, and there is a great scarcity of professors. A commencement was held, nevertheless, this summer, and seven gentlemen took degrees. There are in it at this time about twenty-five students. The president, Dr. Johnson, is a very worthy and learned man, but rather too far advanced in life to have the direction of so young an institution. The late Dr. Bristow left to this college a fine library, of which they are in daily expectation.

The inhabitants of New York, in their character, very much resemble the Pennsylvanians: more than half of them are Dutch, and almost all traders: they are, therefore, habitually frugal, industrious, and parsimonious. Being however of different nations, different languages, and different religions, it is almost impossible to give them any precise or determinate character. The women are handsome and agreeable; though rather more reserved than the Philadelphian ladies. Their amusements are much the same as in Pennsylvania; viz balls, and sleighing expeditions in the winter; and, in the summer, going in parties upon the water, and fishing; or making excursions into the country. There are several houses pleasantly situated upon the East river, near New York, where it is common to have turtle-feasts: these happen once or twice in a week. Thirty or forty gentlemen and ladies meet and dine together, drink tea in the afternoon, fish and amuse themselves till evening, and then return home in Italian chaises, (the fashionable carriage in this and most parts of America, Virginia excepted, where they make use only of coaches, and these commonly drawn by six horses), a gentleman and lady in each chaise. In the way there is a bridge, about three miles distant from New York, which you always pass over as you return, called the Kissing-Bridge, where it is a part of the etiquette to salute the lady who has put herself under your protection.

1770's

From A SNOW STORM IN THE COUNTRY
by St. John de Crèvecoeur

St. John de Crèvecoeur was a Frenchman who came to the American colonies around 1759 looking for adventure. He married a Yonkers girl, Mehetable Tippet, and settled down with her on a farm, "Pine Hill," in upper New York State. The community in which they lived was made up of people of English, Dutch and French descent, independent farmers for the most part. They lived a simple, self-sustaining country life in which husband and wife took an equal share. He was in charge of the outdoors, the planting and harvesting of crops which had to feed family, servants and farm animals. If there were repairs to be made, it was he who had to oversee them, and it was his responsibility to see that enough wood was chopped and hauled to fuel the stove and supply the fireplaces. She carded wool, spun it into cloth, and made clothes for everyone on the farm; and it was her province to cook and can enough food to furnish her family with a dependable food supply during the long winters.

It was a good life. Mr. de Crèvecoeur, who had spent his childhood and youth in a country where great inequalities existed between the rich at one end of the social scale and the poor at the other end, was deeply appreciative of the new, free, democratic American life. The rich Europeans stayed home; it was the middle classes and the poor that emigrated. "A European, when he first arrives, seems limited in his intentions as well as in his views," de Crèvecoeur wrote, "but he very soon alters his scale. . . . He begins to feel the effects of a sort of resurrection; hitherto he had not lived, but simply vegetated; he now feels himself a man, because he is treated as such. . . . He begins to forget his former servitude and dependence, his heart involuntarily dilates and glows, and his first swell inspires him with those new thoughts which make an American."

Of all the scenes which this climate offers, none has struck me with a greater degree of admiration than the ushering in of our winters, and the vehemence with which their first rigor seizes and covers the earth.

A general alarm is spread through the farm. The master calls all his hands; opens the gates; lets down the bars, calls and counts all his stock as they come along. The oxen, the cows, remembering ancient experience, repair to the place where they were foddered the preceding winter; the colts wild, whilst they could unrestrained bound on the grassy fields, suddenly deprived of that liberty, become tame and docile to the hands which stroke and feed them. The sheep, more encumbered than the rest, slowly creep along, and by their incessant bleating show their instinctive apprehension; they are generally the first which attract our attention and care. The horses are led to their stables; the oxen to their stalls; the rest are confined under their proper sheds and districts. All is safe, all is secured from the inclemency of the storm.

At last the farmer returns home loaded with hail and snow melting on his rough but warm clothes. His cheerful wife, not less pleased, welcomes him home with a mug of gingered cider; and whilst she helps him to dried and more comfortable clothes, she recounts to him the successful pains she has taken also in collecting all her ducks, geese, and all the rest of her numerous poultry. But no sooner this simple tale is told than the cheerfulness of her mind is clouded by a sudden thought. Her children went to a distant school early in the morning whilst the sun shone. They are not yet returned. What is to become of them?

These alarming thoughts are soon communicated to her husband who orders one of his negroes to repair to the school with Bonny, the old faithful mare. She is mounted bare-back and hurried through the storm to the schoolhouse, at the door of which each child is impatiently waiting for this paternal assistance. At the sight of honest Tom, the negro, their joy is increased by the pleasure of going home on horseback. One is mounted before and two behind. Thus fixed with difficulty, they turn about and boldly face the driving storm; they all scream and are afraid of falling; at last they clinch together and are hushed.

A joyful meeting ensues. The thoughts of avoided danger increase the pleasure of the family. The milk-biscuit, the short-cake, the newly-baked apple pie are immediately produced, and the sudden joy these presents occasion expels every idea of cold and snow.

Everything is safe both within and without. At that instant the careful negro, Jack, who has been busily employed in carrying wood to the shed that he may not be at a loss to kindle the fire in the morning, comes into his master's room carrying on his hip an enormous back-log. All hands rise; the fire is made to blaze; the hearth is cleaned; and all the cheerful family sit around.

The negroes, friends to the fire, smoke and crack some coarse jokes; and well-fed and clad, they contentedly make their brooms and ladles without any further concerns on their minds. Thus the industrious family, all gathered together, eat their wholesome supper, drink their mugs of cider, and grow less talkative as they grow more sleepy. Finally they go to bed. There, stretched between flannel sheets and covered with warm blankets made of their own sheeps' wool, they enjoy the luxury of sound, undisturbed repose, earned by the fatigues of the preceding day.

Soon after this fall of snow the wind shifts to the northeast and blows with great impetuosity; it gathers and drives the loose element. This second scourge is rather worse than the first, because it renders parts of the road seemingly impassable. 'Tis then that with empty sleighs the neighborhood gathers, and by their united efforts open up a communication along the road. For to live, it is necessary to go to market, to mill, to the woods. This is, besides, the season of merriment and mutual visiting. All the labours of the farm are now reduced to those of the barn; to the fetching of fuel and to cleaning their own flax. Cider is to be found in every house. The convenience of travelling invites the whole country to society, pleasure, and visiting. Bees are made, by which a number of people with their sleighs resort to the inviter's house, and there in one day haul him as much wood as will serve him a whole year. Next day it is another man's turn; admirable contrivance which promotes good-will, kindness, and mutual assistance.

1777

From HOW I WAS ADOPTED BY THE CHIPPEWA
by John Long

JOHN LONG, AN ENGLISHMAN, went to Canada in 1768 as an articled clerk to a Montreal businessman. After he had worked out his seven-year apprenticeship, he led an Indian raiding party for the Loyalists during the early days of the American Revolution. But after two years of war service he left the army and entered the fur trade.

On the fourth of July (1777) we arrived at Pays Plat on the northeast side of the lake (Lake Superior). On our landing we discovered at some distance a number of Indians. They gave me fish, dried meat and skins, which I returned with trifling presents. The chief, whose name was Matchee Quewish held a council, and finding I understood their language, proposed to adopt me as a brother warrior.

The ceremony of adoption is as follows: A feast is prepared of dog's flesh, boiled in bear's grease, with huckleberries, of which it is expected every one should heartily partake. When the repast is over, the war song is sung in the following words:

"Master of Life, view us well: we receive a brother warrior who appears to have sense, shows strength in his arm, and does not refuse his body to the enemy."

After the war song, if the person does not discover any sign of fear, he is regarded with reverence and esteem. Courage, in the opinion of the savages, being considered not only as indispensable, but as the greatest recommendation. He is then seated on a beaver robe and presented with a pipe of war to smoke, which is put round to every warrior, and a wampum belt is thrown over his neck.

When the pipe has gone round, a sweating house is prepared

with six long poles fixed in the ground and pointed at the top. It is then covered with skins and blankets to exclude the air, and the area of the house will contain only three persons. The person to be adopted is then stripped naked, and enters the hut with two chiefs. Two large stones made red-hot are brought in and thrown on the ground; water is then brought in a bark dish and sprinkled on the stones with cedar branches, the steam arising from which puts the person into a most profuse perspiration, and opens the pores to receive the other part of the ceremony.

When the perspiration is at the height, he quits the house and jumps into the water. Immediately on coming out a blanket is thrown over him, and he is led to the chief's hut, where he undergoes the following operation: Being extended on his back, the chief draws the figure he intends to make with a pointed stick, dipped in water on which gunpowder has been dissolved; after which with ten needles dipped in vermilion, and fixed in a small wooden frame, he pricks the delineated parts, and where the bolder outlines occur, he incises the flesh with a gun-flint. The vacant spaces, or those not marked with vermilion, are rubbed in with gunpowder, which produces the variety of red and blue; the wounds are then seared with punk-wood to prevent them from festering.

The operation which is performed at intervals, lasts two or three days. Every morning the parts are washed with cold water in which is infused an herb called *Puckqueesegan,* which resembles English box, and is mixed by the Indians with the tobacco they smoke, to take off the strength. During the process, the war songs are sung, accompanied by a rattle hung round with hawk-bills, called *chessaquoy,* which is kept shaking to stifle the groans such pains must naturally occasion. Upon the ceremony being completed, they give the party a name; that which they allotted to me, was *Amik,* or Beaver.

In return for the presents given me by Matchee Quewish—and

to show how much I was pleased with the honour they had conferred on me, I resolved to add to my former gifts. I accordingly took the chiefs to a spot where I had directed my men to place the goods intended for them, and gave them scalping-knifes, tomahawks, vermilion, tobacco, beads etc., and lastly rum, the *unum necessarium* without which (whatever else had been bestowed on them) I should have incurred their serious displeasure. Our canoes having been turned up, and the goods properly secured, I told the Canadians to keep a constant watch, night and day, while we were encamped. This precaution is absolutely necessary as the Indians generally do mischief when they are intoxicated. On this occasion with the rum we gave them they continued in a state of inebriety three days and nights, during which frolic they killed four of their own party; one of whom was a great chief, and was burnt by his son. Having been a famous warrior, he was buried with the usual honours peculiar to the savages, viz, a scalping knife, tomahawk, beads, paint, etc., some pieces of wood to make a fire, and a bark cup to drink out of in his journey to the other country.

1777

FIRST IMPRESSIONS OF AMERICA
by General Marie Joseph Paul, Marquis de Lafayette

MARIE JOSEPH PAUL, Marquis de Lafayette, was not quite twenty-one years old when, with a small band of other ardent young Frenchmen, he landed at Georgetown, South Carolina, in a ship he had himself chartered and equipped. Almost immediately after arriving in America he traveled to Philadelphia, where he offered his services to the American cause. Congress made him a major general, but without pay and without command. However, Washington liked the young French officer and soon appointed him to his staff. Although the British nicknamed Lafayette "the boy," he fought gallantly both on the field of battle and the field of diplomacy for the liberal American ideals which he so much admired.

The letter that follows was written by Lafayette soon after his arrival in America to his wife, Adrienne de Noaille Lafayette, whom he had married at the age of sixteen.

Charleston, 19 June, 1777

My last letter to you, my dear love, has informed you that I arrived safely in this country, after having suffered a little from sea-sickness during the first weeks of the voyage; that I was then, the morning after I landed, at the house of a very kind officer; that I had been nearly two months on the passage, and that I wished to set off immediately. It spoke of everything most interesting to my heart; of my sorrow at parting from you, and of our dear children; and it said besides that I was in excellent health. I give you this abstract of it, because the English may possibly amuse themselves by seizing it on its way. I landed after having sailed several days along a coast which swarmed with hostile vessels. When I arrived, everybody said that my vessel must inevitably be taken, since two British frigates blocked the harbour. I even went so far as to send orders to the captain, both by land and sea, to put the men on shore and set fire to the ship, if not yet too late. By a most wonderful good fortune, a gale obliged the frigates to stand out to sea for a short time. My vessel came in at noon to-day, without meeting friend or foe.

At Charleston I have met General Howe, an American officer now in the service. The Governor of the State is expected this evening from the country. All with whom I wished to become acquainted here have shown me the greatest politeness and attention.

I feel entirely satisfied with my reception, although I have not thought it best to go into any detail respecting my arrangements and plans. I wish first to see Congress. I hope to set out for Philadelphia in two days. Our route is more than two hundred and fifty leagues by land. Some French and American vessels are here, and are to sail together to-morrow morning, taking advantage of a moment when the frigates are out of sight. They are armed, and have promised me to defend themselves stoutly against the small privateers, which they will certainly meet. I shall distribute my letters among the different ships.

I will now tell you about the country and its inhabitants. They are as agreeable as my enthusiasm had painted them. Simplicity of manners, kindness, love of country and of liberty, and a delightful equality everywhere prevail. The wealthiest man and the poorest are on a level; and, although there are some large fortunes, I challenge anyone to discover the slightest difference between the manners of these two classes respectively towards each other. I first saw the country life at the house of Major Huger. I am now in the city, where everything is very much after the English fashion, except that there is more simplicity, equality, cordiality, and courtesy, here than in England. The city of Charleston is one of the handsomest and best built, and its inhabitants are the most agreeable that I have ever seen. The American women are very pretty, simple in their manners, and exhibit a neatness, which is everywhere cultivated even more studiously than in England. What most charms me is, that all the citizens are brethren. In America, there are no poor, nor even what we call peasantry. Each individual has his own honest property, and the same rights as the most wealthy landed proprietor. The inns are very different from those of Europe; the host and hostess sit at table with you, and do the honours of a comfortable meal; and, on going away, you pay your bill without haggling. When one does not wish to go to an inn, there are country-houses where the title of a good American is a sufficient passport to all those civilities paid in Europe to one's friend.

As to my own reception, it has been most agreeable in every quarter: I have just passed five hours at a grand dinner, given in honour of me by an individual of this city. Generals Howe and Moultrie, and several officers of my suite were present. We drank health and tried to talk English. I begin to speak it a little. To-morrow I shall go with these gentlemen to call on the Governor of the State, and make arrangements for my departure. The next day the commanding officers here will show me the city and its environs, and then I shall set out for the army.

Remember me to your friends and my own, to the dear society, once the society of the court, but which by the lapse of time has become the society of the Wooden Sword. We republicans think it all the better. I must leave off for want of paper and time; and if I do not repeat to you ten thousand times that I love you, it is not from any want of feeling, but from modesty; since I have the presumption to hope, that I have already convinced you of it. The night is far advanced, and the heat dreadful. I am devoured by insects; so, you see, the best countries have their disadvantages. Adieu.

1777

THE SURRENDER OF BURGOYNE
by Madame de Riedesel

BARONESS FREDERICKA CHARLOTTE LOUISE RIEDESEL and her three
little children accompanied her husband, General Friederich
Adolph Riedesel, when that Hessian officer was sent to America in
command of a division of German soldiers. Baroness Riedesel, as
well as her children, were present when the British General John
Burgoyne, together with the German regiments attached to his
command, surrendered to the Americans on October 17th, 1777,
near Saratoga. The victory gave a much needed lift to the American
morale, immobilized a quarter of the invading armies, and put control of the Hudson River permanently in American hands.

We were halted at six o'clock in the morning [Oct. 9, 1777] to our
general amazement. General Burgoyne ordered the artillery to be
drawn up in a line, and to have it counted. This gave much dis-
satisfaction, as a few marches more would have ensured our safety.
My husband was exhausted by fatigue, and took a seat in the calash,
where my maids made room for him; and he slept for three hours
upon my shoulder. In the mean time, Captain Willoe brought me his
pocket-book containing bank-notes, and Captain Geismar, a beautiful
watch, a ring, and a well-provided purse, requesting me to keep them,
which I promised to do to the last. At length we recommenced our
march; but scarcely an hour had elapsed, before the army was again
halted, because the enemy was in sight. They were but two hundred
in number, who came to reconnoitre, and who might easily have
been taken, had not general Burgoyne lost all his presence of mind.
The rain fell in torrents. On the 9th, it rained terribly the whole
day; nevertheless we kept ourselves ready to march. The savages had
lost their courage, and they walked off in all directions. The least

untoward event made them dispirited, especially when there was no opportunity for plunder. My chambermaid exclaimed the whole day against her fate, and seemed mad with despair. I begged her to be quiet, unless she wished to be taken for a savage. "You can take it quite easily," said she, "for you have your husband; but we have nothing but the prospect of being killed, or of losing the little we possess."

We reached Saratoga about dark, which was but half an hour's march from the place where we had spent the day. I was quite wet, and was obliged to remain in that condition, for want of a place to change my apparel. I seated myself near the fire, and undressed the children, and we then laid ourselves upon some straw.—I asked general Phillips, who came to see how I was, why we did not continue our retreat, my husband having pledged himself to cover the movement, and to bring off the army in safety. "My poor lady," said he, "you astonish me. Though quite wet, you have so much courage as to wish to go further in this weather. What a pity it is that you are not our commanding general! He complains of fatigue, and has determined upon spending the night here, and giving us a supper." It is very true, that general Burgoyne liked to make himself easy, and that he spent half the nights in drinking and diverting himself. I refreshed myself at 7 o'clock the next morning with a cup of tea, and we all expected that we should soon continue our march. About 2 o'clock, we heard again a report of muskets and cannon, and there was much alarm and bustle among our troops. My husband sent me word, that I should immediately retire into a house which was not far off. I got into my calash with my children, and when we were near the house I saw, on the opposite bank of the Hudson, five or six men, who aimed at us with their guns. Without knowing what I did, I threw my children into the back part of the vehicle, and laid myself upon them. At the same moment the fellow fired, and broke the arm of a poor English soldier, who stood behind us, and who being already wounded, sought a shelter. Soon after our arrival, a terrible cannonade began, and the fire was principally directed against the house, where we had hoped to find a refuge, probably because the enemy inferred, from the great number of people who went towards it, that this was the headquarters of the generals, while, in reality, none were there except women and crippled soldiers. We were at last obliged to descend into the cellar, where I laid myself in a corner near the door. My children put their heads upon my knees. An abominable smell, the cries of the children, and my own anguish of mind, did not permit me to close my eyes, during the whole night. On the next morning, the cannonade began anew, but in a different direction. Eleven cannon-balls passed through the house, and made a tremendous noise. A poor soldier, who was about to have a leg amputated, lost the other one by one of these balls. All his comrades ran away at that moment, and when they returned, they found him in one corner of the room, in the agonies of death. I was myself in the deepest distress, not so much on account of my own dangers, as of those to which my husband was exposed, who, however, frequently sent me messages, inquiring after my health.

The want of water continuing to distress us, we could not but be extremely glad to find a soldier's wife so spirited as to fetch some from the river, an occupation from which the boldest might have shrunk, as the Americans shot every one who approached it. They told us afterwards that they spared her on account of her sex.

On the 17th of October, the capitulation was carried into effect. The generals waited upon the American General Gates, and the troops surrendered themselves prisoners of war and laid down their arms. The time had now come for the good woman who had risked her life to supply us with water, to receive the reward of her services. Each of us threw a handful of money into her apron; and she thus received more than twenty guineas. At such a moment at least, if at no other, the heart easily overflows with gratitude.

At last my husband's groom brought me a message to join him with the children. I once more seated myself in my dear calash, and, while riding through the American camp, was gratified to observe that nobody looked at us with disrespect, but, on the contrary, greeted us, and seemed touched at the sight of a captive mother with three children. I must candidly confess that I did not present myself, though so situated, with much courage to the enemy, for the thing was entirely new to me. When I drew near the tents, a good looking man advanced towards me, and helped the children from the calash, and kissed and caressed them: he then offered me his arm, and tears trembled in his eyes. "You tremble," said he; "do not be alarmed, I pray you." "Sir," cried I, "a countenance so expressive of benevolence, and the kindness which you have evinced towards my children, are sufficient to dispel all apprehension." He then ushered me into the tent of general Gates.

The gentleman who had received me with so much kindness came and said to me, "You may find it embarrassing to be the only lady in such a large company of gentlemen; will you come with your children to my tent, and partake of a frugal dinner, offered with the best will?" "By the kindness you show to me," returned I, "you induce me to believe that you have a wife and children." He informed me that he was general Schuyler. He regaled me with smoked tongues, which were excellent, with beefsteaks, potatoes, fresh butter and bread. Never did a dinner give me so much pleasure as this. I was easy, after many months of anxiety, and I read the same happy change in the countenances of those around me.

1779

GENERAL GEORGE WASHINGTON
by François, Marquis de Barbé-Marbois

FRANÇOIS, MARQUIS DE BARBÉ-MARBOIS was thirty-four years old when he was sent to America in 1779 to be Secretary of the French Legation. At the end of the Revolution when the Ambassador, the Chevalier de la Lucerne, left for home, Barbé-Marbois was promoted to chargé d'affaires and represented France to the United States government until 1785 when he was made governor of Santo Domingo.

The excerpt that follows is taken from a letter he wrote home to his fiancée. (He later broke their engagement to marry an American girl.)

September (1779)

We continued our journey through Greenfield, Stratford, and Fairfield, whose name indicates its natural beauty. But we could not see without pity the condition of this country, which the English swept over, with fire and sword in their hands, two months ago. For a distance of two leagues almost all the dwellings were burned completely. Since they were built entirely of wood, except for the fireplaces and chimneys, you see a mass of isolated bricks twenty-five to thirty feet high, which alone has escaped the flames. Americans who have the courage to joke even about their misfortunes call these ruins "English chimneys."

In spite of all the objections of M. de la Luzerne [the French Ambassador], General Washington came to meet him at Fishkill. He received us with a noble, modest, and gentle urbanity and with the graciousness which seems to be the basis of his character. He is fifty years old, well built, rather thin. He carries himself freely and with a sort of military grace. He is masculine-looking, without his features being less gentle on that account. I have never seen anyone who was more naturally and spontaneously polite. His eyes are blue and rather large, his mouth and nose are regular, and his forehead open. His uniform is exactly like that of his soldiers. Formerly, on solemn occasions, that is to say on days of battles, he wore a large blue sash, but he has given up that unrepublican distinction. I have seen him for some time in the midst of his staff, and he has always appeared even-tempered, tranquil, and orderly in his occupations, and serious in his conversation. He asks few questions, listens attentively, and answers in a low tone with a few words. He is serious in business. Outside of that, he permits himself a restricted gaiety. His conversation is as simple as his habits and his appearance. He makes no pretensions and does the honors of his house with dignity, but without pompousness or flattery. He sometimes throws and catches a ball for whole hours with his aides de camp. He is reverent without bigotry, and abhors swearing, which he punishes with the greatest severity.

We embarked with the General on the North River, or the Hudson, and sailed down it with the tide to West Point where the headquarters are, surrounded by the chief posts of the American army. The general held the tiller, and during a little squall which required skill and practise, proved to us that this work was no less known to him than are other bits of useful knowledge.

During dinner the general told me that he was drinking the health of the Marquis de Lafayette, and asked if I had seen him before my departure. I answered that I had, and added that he spoke of him with the tenderest veneration. I said that the conduct of M. de Lafayette in America had made him generally esteemed, and caused him to deserve the distinction and favor granted him by the King. Washington blushed like a fond father whose child is being praised. Tears fell from his eyes, he clasped my hand, and could hardly utter the words: "I do not know a nobler, finer soul, and I love him as my own son."

At nine in the morning we got on horses to accompany the General who wanted to conduct us himself to all the chief posts of the position which he has taken up on the Hudson. I walked near the general, and in the course of the conversation, I asked him if he would not come to France some day, and enjoy the plaudits of a responsive nation which idolizes glory. He told me that he was only waiting for the end of the war to retire to his estates and finish out his days there in the bosom of his family, after having paid the debt which every citizen owes to his country in times of trouble and misfortune.

1780

From A LETTER FROM NEW YORK
by a Hessian Officer

IN 1776 THE HEREDITARY PRINCE OF HESSE-CASSEL found himself in need of money. At the same time, His Majesty George III of England needed soldiers to help him fight his rebelling American colonists. In their mutual need the two rulers got together and signed a contract in which the Prince of Hesse-Cassel agreed to furnish the English "668 men in good health, equipped with tents and all necessary equipage and ready to march" and, in return, George III promised to pay "to His Most Serene Highness for each foot soldier thirty crowns banco; according to custom, three wounded men shall be reckoned as one killed: a man killed shall be paid at the rate of the levy money."

Drafted and shipped out of the country like cattle, the Hessian regiments, though only hired soldiers, fought well and bravely in support of the British troops.

September 11, 1780

Washington is on the North River in our vicinity and is cutting all kinds of capers, which no one bothers about. In the remote interior of the country a certain *Johnson, Butler,* and others with a party of royalists and Indians are busy burning, murdering, plundering, taking prisoners, and whatever other such little war-plays there may be: are making themselves terrible to the inhabitants, who live singly and scattered, and their residence dangerous. Meanwhile the spirit of rebellion in Philadelphia and around us is not yet weary of forcing the inhabitants to arms by flattery, deception, threats, and open violence, and of continuing the war; despite the fact that their finances, their credit, and their money sink lower and lower daily. Only last spring the Congress vainly sought to raise the value of the paper money; but it has already fallen one half again: eighty or ninety paper dollars for one of silver.

At first I was inclined to be favorable to the Americans. Prejudices and false conceptions of the oppression threatening them—with which our German papers always embellished their cause—brought me on their side. But since I have had a chance to get closer acquainted with their history, their motives for the war, and their character as a whole, I have no further wishes for them. The most abominable trait in their make-up is ingratitude. It is true, when I tell you how happy, unconcerned, and quiet they lived in the lap of the most beneficent Nature before the outbreak of these unhappy disturbances; so one is almost inclined to recognize the British as tyrants who cannot bear to see their offspring happy; and so they picture it to you. But let some one calculate for you, on the other hand, the unstinted care with which the mother country watched over its colonies from their origin; the severe and costly wars it fought, now with the Indians, now with neighboring European nations, for the sake of this safety and quiet—whereby the Americans, for the most part, calmly looked on; the other great sums which it spent on their inner civil arrangements, salaries, churches, schools, academies, etc., etc.; and then, when it was asked, as was right and proper, that they should take upon their shoulders a part of these burdens heaped up on their account—then the child rebelled against its mother. But all the pretext of resistance to the imposition of illegal taxes was in the beginning nothing more than a mask, a trumped up reason. The plan for that rebellion is laid older and deeper and was conceived and hatched chiefly in the New England provinces. Since this sort of people are mostly Presbyterians and Puritans, so for a long time—in accord with their church principles—all secular authority, but especially the name and power of the king, has been a thorn in their eye. The New Englanders for years bore the name of *Yenkies* and were always known in all the provinces as crafty folk, deceitful under their mask of holiness.

1780

From A REPORT DRAWN UP IN PRISON
by Major John André

THE STORY OF MAJOR JOHN ANDRÉ, Adjutant General of the British Army, is one of the saddest episodes of the American Revolution. Thirty years old, handsome, popular and witty, André was sent by his superior officer, Sir Henry Clinton, on a mission which he himself had opposed but felt he must undertake because he was a British officer whose duty it was to carry out orders.

In 1780 General Benedict Arnold was in command of West Point where he had made a plan to surrender that fort to the British. Major André was to take charge of the negotiations. Wearing his uniform, André was landed near West Point from the *Vulture*, a British sloop. He had his talk with General Arnold but was prevented from rejoining the *Vulture* according to plan because the boat had been forced to retire under American gunfire. André spent the night at a farmhouse. The next morning he changed into civilian dress, made an attempt to reach the British lines by land, and was caught near Tarrytown. He was subsequently tried by a Court of General Officers of which Lafayette was a member, and was found guilty. He was hanged as a spy on October 2nd, 1780.

On the 20th of September, I left New York to get on board the Vulture, in order (as I thought) to meet General Arnold there in the night. No boat, however, came off, and I waited on board until the night of the 21st. During the day, a flag of truce was sent from the Vulture to complain of the violation of a military rule in the instance of a boat having been decoyed on shore by a flag, and fired upon. The letter was addressed to general Arnold, signed by Captain Sutherland, but written in my hand and countersigned 'J. Anderson, secretary.' Its intent was to indicate my presence on board the Vulture. In the night of the 21st a boat with Mr. (Smith) and two hands came on board, in order to fetch Mr. Anderson on shore, and, if too late, to bring me back, to lodge me until the next night in a place of safety. I went into the boat, landed, and spoke with Arnold. I got on horseback with him to proceed to (Smith's) house, and in the way passed a guard I did not expect to see, having Sir Clinton's directions not to go within an enemy's post, or to quit my own dress.

In the morning A. quitted me, having himself made me put the papers I bore between my stockings and feet. Whilst he did it, he expressed a wish in case of any accident befalling me, that they should be destroyed, which I said, of course would be the case, as when I went into the boat I should have them tied about with a string and a stone. Before we parted, some mention had been made of my crossing the river, and going by another route; but, I objected much against it, and thought it was settled that in the way I came I was also to return.

Mr. (Smith), to my great mortification, persisted in his determination of carrying me by the other route; and, at the decline of the sun, I set out on horseback, passed King's Ferry, and came to Crompond, where a party of militia stopped us and advised we should remain. In the morning I came with (Smith) as far as within two miles and a half of Pine's Bridge, where he said he must part with me, as the Cow-boys infested the road thence forward. I was now near thirty miles from Kingsbridge, and left to the chance of passing that space undiscovered. I got to the neighborhood of Tarrytown, which was far beyond the points described as dangerous, when I was taken by three volunteers, who, not satisfied with my pass, rifled me, and, finding papers, made me a prisoner.

I have omitted mentioning, that, when I found myself within an enemy's post, I changed my dress.

Failing in an appeal for clemency, Major André resigned himself to death. The day before his execution, he wrote the following letter to General Washington. The request he made was denied, and he died on the gallows.

Tappan, 1 October, 1780— Sir; Buoyed above the terror of death, by the consciousness of a life devoted to honorable pursuits, and stained with no action that can give me remorse, I trust that the request I make to your Excellency at this serious period, and which is to soften my last moments, will not be rejected.

Sympathy towards a soldier will surely induce your Excellency and a military tribunal to adapt the mode of my death to the feelings of a man of honor.

Let me hope, Sir, that if aught in my character impresses you with esteem towards me, if aught in my misfortunes marks me as the victim of policy and not of resentment, I shall experience the opera-

tion of these feelings in your breast, by being informed that I am not
to die on a gibbet.

I have the honor to be your Excellency's most obedient and most
humble servant.

John André
Adj. Gen. to the British Army

1781

SURRENDER AT YORKTOWN
by Charles, First Marquis Cornwallis

EXACTLY FOUR YEARS after Burgoyne's surrender at Saratoga another
British army, led this time by General Cornwallis, was forced to lay
down its arms at Yorktown.

Early in August 1781, Cornwallis and his troops, harassed by
colonial forces, had moved down the York River to entrench themselves at Yorktown. By the end of August, Washington had sent
an army of combined American and French troops to lay siege to
the British forces and a French fleet under Admiral de Grasse had
dropped anchor at the mouth of the York River to prevent Cornwallis from escaping by sea and to bar the arrival of reinforcements.

At the outbreak of hostilities, Cornwallis in England had
openly said that he was opposed to war with the colonies, but he
was an able and honest general and he had been sent to America
in spite of his convictions. At Yorktown he was outnumbered and
outmaneuvered by Washington and his mixed army of French and
colonial troops.

Day after day the allied troops stormed Cornwallis's outer
redoubts and broke down his inner defenses with their gunfire. On
October 17th, when he had only one hundred shells left and his
men were sick and exhausted, Cornwallis bowed to the inevitable
and ran up the white flag. The official surrender took place on

October 19th, and with this British defeat the Americans had won their Revolution.

Yorktown was the last battle of the war, and although a peace treaty was not actually signed until September 3rd, 1783, the Yorktown disaster broke the will of the British to continue fighting and marked the end of hostilities between the opposing armies.

Yorktown, Virginia, Oct. 20, 1781

I have the mortification to inform your Excellency that I have been forced to give up the posts of York and Gloucester, and to surrender the troops under my command, by capitulation, on the 19th instant, as prisoners of war to the combined forces of America and France.

Our works were going to ruin, and not having been able to strengthen them by an abattis, nor in any other manner but by a slight fraizing, which the enemy's artillery were demolishing wherever they fired, my opinion entirely coincided with that of the engineer and principal officers of the army, that they were in many places assailable in the forenoon, and that by the continuance of the same fire for a few hours longer, they would be in such a state as to render it desperate, with our numbers, to attempt to maintain them. We at that time could not fire a single gun; only one 8-inch and little more than 100 Cohorn shells remained. A diversion by the French ships of war that lay at the mouth of York River was to be expected. Our numbers had been diminished by the enemy's fire, but particularly by sickness, and the strength and spirits of those in the works were much exhausted, by the fatigue of constant watching and unremitting duty. Under all these circumstances, I thought it would have been wanton and inhuman to the last degree to sacrifice the lives of this small body of gallant soldiers, who had ever behaved with so much fidelity and courage, by exposing them to an assault which, from the numbers and precautions of the enemy, could not fail to succeed. I therefore proposed to capitulate; and I have the honour to enclose to your Excellency the copy of the correspondence between general Washington and me on that subject, and the terms of the capitulation agreed upon. I sincerely lament that better could not be obtained, but I have neglected nothing in my power to alleviate the misfortune and distress of both officers and soldiers. The men are well clothed and provided with necessaries, and I trust will be regularly supplied by the means of the officers that are permitted to remain with them. The treatment, in general, that we have received from the enemy since our surrender has been perfectly good and proper, but the kindness and attention that has been shown to us by the French officers in particular—their delicate sensibility of our situation—their generous and pressing offer of money, both public and private, to any amount—has really gone beyond what I can possibly describe, and will, I hope, make an impression on the breast of every British officer, whenever the fortune of war should put any of them into our power.

1781

THE SURRENDER AT YORKTOWN
by Baron Ludwig von Closen

BARON LUDWIG VON CLOSEN was born in The Palatinate but moved to France at an early age and thereafter gave his whole-souled allegiance to his adopted country. He came to America as aide-de-camp to General Rochambeau and was with him at Yorktown where as captain of an infantry regiment he showed courage under fire. Blond and blue-eyed, von Closen was a gay and gallant figure. He was also an excellent linguist and often served as interpreter at conferences.

19, Oct., 1781

At two o'clock the garrison of York marched past the combined army, which was drawn up in two lines, the French in full dress opposite the Americans. The captive army laid its arms and 22 flags on a designated spot at the end of the line, where the general staff of the army received them. The Gloucester garrison did the same before M. de Choisy.

Lord Cornwallis, under the pretext of an indisposition, excused himself from this sad ceremony, so that Brigadier-General O'Hara marched at the head of the English troops. In passing between the two armies, they showed the greatest scorn for the Americans, who, to tell the truth, were eclipsed by our army in splendor of appearance and dress, for most of these unfortunate persons were clad in small jackets of white cloth, dirty and ragged, and a number of them were almost barefoot. The English had given them the *nickname* of "Janckey-dudle." What does it matter! An intelligent man would say. These people are much more praise-worthy and brave to fight as they do, when they are so poorly supplied with everything.

20, Oct., 1781

We found Lord Cornwallis at his residence. His appearance gave the impression of nobility of soul, magnanimity, and strength of character; his manner seemed to say, "I have nothing with which to reproach myself, I have done my duty, and I held out as long as possible."

1785

A VISIT TO AMERICA
From the Diary of Joseph Hadfield

JOSEPH HADFIELD was a young Englishman who came to America just two years after the close of the War of Independence. The object of his trip was to try to collect some prewar debts owed by American businessmen to a firm of Manchester merchants with which Joseph Hadfield's family was connected.

In 1785, the young American democracy was still licking its wounds. Times were hard, life was primitive, and traveling was arduous. But Joseph Hadfield, young, enterprising and well supplied with letters of introduction, stayed the better part of a year, combining business with pleasure and journeying from Virginia to Canada and back again via the New England states.

We made the coast of America near Cape Charles and Cape Henry which is the opening of the Chesapeake in Virginia. The land is low and flat, and for some distance the trees appear to be growing in the sea. We entered the Bay and capes and landed at Yorktown, too celebrated by the capture of Lord Cornwallis and his army.

I could perceive a malignant joy amongst the Americans when we Englishmen were reminded of the above unfortunate disgrace of the British arms which was only equaled by that of Burgoyne at Saratoga.

As I was desirous of seeing Norfolk, I took my passage in a ferry boat which crossed James River which, some miles wide, enters into Elizabeth River on which the town is situated. It was a place of great commerce before the war, but was like many others burnt and destroyed in the sanguinary and unnatural contest with the enemy. Both sides were guilty of great excesses and cruelties. So much does civil dissension destroy humanity and even natural connections and sympathies. For, as in the time of Charles I and Cromwell, families were disunited, parents and children in arms against each other.

I saw nothing but ruins around me. Some people were repairing their houses and others living in sheds and outhouses. The only tavern, if it could be so-called, was wretched and crowded with a motley and noisy set of beings, many by their conduct and appearance half savage, nay worse than the Indian tribes. Englishmen were constantly liable to insult, and it required great forbearance, and nothing but submission to all passing scenes could protect us from violence.

Refreshments were difficult to be procured, everything exorbitantly charged for, and no comfort. Everyone came in and out at pleasure and the long-legged Virginia planters, as tall as maypoles, as ill-shaped as the branches of an oak, would, without ceremony, help themselves to any bowl of a stranger's toddy (which is rum and water with sugar) and make no apology. I was now to look out for a bed to pass the night, fully determined it should be the last in that habitation. But here I found a difficulty as there were more applications than could be sufficed. However, I determined to make friends with the females of the house, making use of all my eloquence which at least produced a promise that I should have half a bed in a large barn. This I declined without I might have it to myself. I found I must take my chance of being intruded upon.

Never shall I forget when I was shown to a straw palisse with blankets and no sheets. I am sure the floor of this large outhouse was covered with twenty such beds and men. I was the first to retire to my berth near the boards, through which the winds whistled. But notwithstanding this, overcome by fatigue, I was soon fast asleep. In the night I was awakened by a drunken fellow staggering over me, and who would have stopped if I had not forced him away. Now I heard the vociferations of a party of Virginians gaming in an adjoining building. From words they got to blows. All was confusion, a perfect

Hell if swearing and excesses could make it so. I found I would have no repose, and not having undressed, I got out of the room and walked in the open air until it was light, when I made inquiries for some conveyance over the river to York or Williamsburgh. Two persons joined me in hiring an open boat to be rowed by two negroes.

We had scarce got half way over the river when the boat leaked and the water came in so fast that it required our united exertions to prevent sinking. We were obliged to make use of our hats to get rid of the water. We got to a small uninhabited island where we rested and then intended to land near Williamsburgh. But sundry impediments prevented us and we were at last benighted and with difficulty landed.

We climbed up the banks in search of a house, but it was some time before we found one, and that at least a mile from the river. The people were in bed, and after knocking, a man opened the window, put out a gun and threatened to shoot us if we did not go away. We then went in search of a more hospitable dwelling which we found at last in a plantation, but so poor that he could only give us a piece of hoe-cake, made of Indian corn, such as they feed the negroes with. However, hunger made us relish it. I waited with impatience until morning when I was fortunate enough to hire a horse and guide to conduct me to Williamsburgh, about 5 or 6 miles distant.

I had time during the few days I remained to examine the town which was the residence of Lord Dunmore when Governor, and the seat of Government, which had since been removed. The place was almost devastated, but the buildings were superior to what I had seen. I saw with concern the ravages of war wherever I went, and one cannot be surprised that the people who were preyed upon by friends as well as foes should be soured by their losses.

I heard no other subject but curses upon the English Government and armies. Whoever visited America at this period and expected to find the country and cultivation like England would be sadly disappointed. You find noble and majestic trees in forests upon a wild plain, with tobacco and Indian corn and some small lean wheat etc. The fences are made with split trees about 15 feet long and laid cross-ways on each other like a Vandyke collar. The sameness when compared with our briar hedges is disagreeable. The rivers are large and numerous. In this America surpasses Europe where the rivers are mere streamlets. Nothing can exceed the vast expanse of these inland water communications but they are more grand than beautiful.

The roads are very bad, and of a dull, monotonous appearance. The planters—and upon these lower parts of Virginia are many gentlemen—have handsome houses, and according to their estates, numerous gangs of negroes. You can see these negroes employed by men who have been fighting for Independence, whilst they themselves keep thousands in slavery.

Among the many inconveniences I experienced in travelling, that of the venomous bites of mosquitoes is dreadful. You are obliged to have veils of gauze and curtains of the same at night. Every part of the human body of strangers is swollen, sometimes to such a degree as to produce fevers. It is impossible to describe my sufferings from them. The ditches and marshes are full of bull-frogs of immense size whose loud and discordant croakings may be heard at a great distance. I may with truth remark that from my landing at Yorktown until I arrived at Philadelphia, I had to encounter every physical and mental misery that a human being could be exposed to.

GROWTH OF A NEW NATION

1796

A MEETING WITH DANIEL BOONE
by Francis Baily

FRANCIS BAILY, in later life a distinguished British astronomer, Fellow of the Royal Society and member of the Linnian and Geological Societies as well, was a young man of twenty-two out of a job when he came to America in 1796. He stayed in the United States two years, covering a great portion of the country, including much of the western section. Young, adventurous and observant, he rejected the usual tourist-type modes of travel, "passed eleven months without the shelter of a civilized roof," and with a friend cruised in an open boat down the Ohio and Mississippi rivers. It was on this journey that Baily met up with an "Old Colonel Boone" who turned out to be none other than the famous Daniel.

Returning to England, Baily became a successful stockbroker. For a long while his scientific work was more an avocation than a vocation. But in 1825, having made a considerable amount of money, he decided that intellectual work meant more to him than worldly success and he retired from the Stock Exchange. From this time until his death he devoted himself entirely to scientific research both in astronomy and in general science.

Sunday, April 9th. We had observed a canoe ahead of us the preceding day, and for the sake of company wished we could have overtaken it; but as the person who was in it did not seem disposed to stop for us, we soon lost sight of him, as he proceeded along much faster than we. However, this morning we observed the same vessel behind us, and in a short time it came alongside. It contained but one old man, accompanied by his dog and his gun, and a few things lying at the bottom of the canoe. We called to him to come into our boat, which he accordingly did; and after a little conversation, our guest proved to be old Colonel Boone, the first discoverer of the now flourishing state of Kentucky. I was extremely happy in having an opportunity of conversing with the hero of so many adventures, a relation of which is drawn up and published in Imlay's Geography. Happening to have this account by me, I read it over to him, and he confirmed all that was there related to him. I could observe the old man's face brighten up at the mention of those transactions in which he had taken so active a part; and upon my adverting particularly to his adventure in August 1778 with the Indians at Boonesborough, where they, with most barefaced deceit, endeavored to take him and his men prisoners, he entered upon the subject with all the minuteness imaginable, and as descriptively as if it had recently happened. He then made us follow him in his narration,—how he was taken prisoner by the Indians, and carried a tour round the lakes with them; and the old man interspersed his tale with many a pleasing anecdote and interesting observation. He took (in truly an Indian style) a drop of water, and on a board he marked out the whole course of his travels; and, though I showed him a map, he continued on, after barely looking at it, and would not be diverted from the one which he had formed with his own finger. Upon asking him whether it did not give him a secret satisfaction to behold a province (in the discovery and settlement of which he held so conspicuous a part) rise from a desert wilderness, and at once to flourish in arts and sciences and the conveniences of life, in all the maturity of old age, he shook his head, and with a significant frown, said they were got too proud;

and then began to enter into the disadvantages of great improvements of society. He said he had a great deal of land given him on the first settlement of the country; but that when societies began to form around him, he moved off, and divided his lands among his relations, unwilling (as he expressed himself) to live among men who were shackled in their habits, and would not enjoy uncontrolled the free blessings which nature had bestowed upon them. Since this time, he told me he had spent his time a great deal on the frontiers; and at this present moment he said he was going to hunt for beavers in some unfrequented corner of the woods, where undisturbed he might pursue this amusement, and enjoy the pleasures arising from a secluded and solitary life.

1798

AN ENCOUNTER WITH GENERAL WASHINGTON
by John Bernard

JOHN BERNARD WAS ONE of the most famous English comedians of his day. He was forty-one years old when he came to Philadelphia, lured by the promise of £1,000 a year [$5,000], a very high salary for those times. With the wit and geniality that made him popular as a man as well as an actor, Bernard hints at financial difficulties as a motive for his American trip. "The causes which led me to make one of the band who were bold enough to face the perils of swamps, snakes, tomahawks, and Yankees in far-off America can be told in a very few words," he writes; "they were the failure of two or three managerial speculations and the patronage of an extensive circle of fashionable acquaintances."

Bernard played in Philadelphia with great success for six years then went to Boston as a joint manager of the Federal Theatre there.

In 1819 he went home to England where he died in 1828.

It was during the Philadelphia period that he had his adventure with George Washington.

A few weeks after my location at Annapolis, I met with a most pleasing adventure, no less than an encounter with General Washington, under circumstances which most fully confirmed the impression I had formed of him. I had been to pay a visit to an acquaintance on the banks of the Potomac, a few miles below Alexandria, and was returning on horse-back in the rear of an old-fashioned chaise, the driver of which was strenuously urging his steed to an accelerated pace. The beast showed singular indifference, till a lash, directed with more skill than humanity, took the skin from an old wound. The sudden pang threw the poor animal on his hind legs, and the wheel swerving upon the bank, over went the chaise, flinging out upon the road a young woman who had been its occupant.

The minute before I had perceived a horse-man approaching at a gentle trot, who now broke into a gallop, and we reached the scene of the disaster together. The female was our first care. She was insensible but had sustained no material injury. My companion supported her, while I brought some water in the crown of my hat, from a spring some way off.

A gush of tears announced the lady's return to sensibility.

The horse was now on its legs but the vehicle still prostrate, heavy in its frame, and laden with at least half a ton of luggage. My fellow-helper set me an example in relieving it of the external weight; and when all was clear, we grasped the wheel between us and to the peril of my spinal column, righted the conveyance. The horse was then put in, and we lent a hand to help up the luggage and when all was right, and we had assisted the lady to resume her seat [they] drove on.

My companion, after an exclamation at the heat, offered very courteously to dust my coat, a favor the return of which enabled me to take a deliberate survey of his person. He was a tall, erect, well-made man, evidently advanced in years, but who appeared to have retained all the vigor and elasticity resulting from a life of temperance and exercise. His dress was a blue coat, buttoned to his chin, and buckskin breeches. Though the instant he took off his hat, I could not avoid the recognition of familiar lineaments—which, indeed, I was in the habit of seeing on every sign-post and over every fire-place—still I failed to identify him, and, to my surprise, I found that I was an object of speculation in his eyes.

A smile at length lighted them up and he exclaimed, "Mr. Bernard, I believe?" I bowed. "I had the pleasure of seeing you perform last winter in Philadelphia." I bowed again, and he added, "I have heard of you since from several of my friends at Annapolis. You must be fatigued. If you will ride up to my home, which is not a mile distant, you can prevent any ill-effects from this exertion, by a couple of hours' rest." I looked around for his dwelling and he pointed to a building which the day before, I had spent an hour in contemplating. "Mount Vernon!" I exclaimed; and then, drawing back, with a stare of wonder, "have I the honor of addressing General Washington?" With a smile whose expression of benevolence I have rarely seen equalled, he offered his hand and replied, "An odd sort of introduction, Mr. Bernard; but I am pleased to find you can play so active a part in private, and without a prompter." As we rode up to his house we entered freely into conversation, first, in reference to friends of his at Annapolis, then respecting my own success in America and the impressions I had received of the country.

Flattering as such inquiries were from such a source, I must confess my own reflections on what had just passed were more absorbing. Considering that nine ordinary country gentlemen out of ten, who had seen a chaise upset near their estate, would have thought it savored neither of pride nor ill-nature to ride home and send their servants to its assistance, I could not but think that I had witnessed one of the strongest evidences of a great man's claim to his reputation —the prompt, impulsive working of a heart which having made the good of mankind—not conventional forms—its religion, was never so happy as in practically displaying it.

1804

THOMAS JEFFERSON
by Sir Augustus John Foster

Sir Augustus John Foster was Secretary of the British Legation in Washington when he met Thomas Jefferson in 1804.

Young, handsome and sophisticated, Foster made the best of Washington society; though, to this much-traveled son of a Duchess, who had already met such European celebrities as Napoleon, Talleyrand, Goethe and Schiller, the social life of the young American capital seemed rather naïve and provincial.

Foster went home to England in 1808 but was sent back to America in 1810, this time as Minister to the United States. The War of 1812 broke out during his term as Minister.

It may be interesting to the reader to have the following description of Thomas Jefferson as he appeared to me on my arrival in the United States in the year 1804. He was a tall man with a very red freckled face and grey neglected hair, his manners good-natured, frank and rather friendly though he had somewhat of a cynical expression of countenance. He wore a blue coat, a thick grey-coloured hairy waistcoat with a red under-waistcoat lapped over it, green velveteen breeches with pearl buttons, yarn stockings and slippers down at the heel, his appearance being very much like that of a tall large-boned farmer.

The family breakfast hour was eight o'clock. After breakfast Mrs. Randolph [Jefferson's daughter] and her amiable daughters as well as the other female relations of the house set about cleaning the tea-things and washing the alabaster lamp, which I took to be designed as a catch for popularity. After this operation the President retired to his books, his daughter to give lessons to her children, her husband to the farm, and the guests were left to amuse themselves as they pleased till four o'clock, walking, riding or shooting. The President took his daily ride at one o'clock to look at his farm and mill, at four dinner was served up, and in the evening we walked on a wooden terrace or strolled into the wood, Mr. Jefferson playing with his grandchildren till dusk when tea was brought in, and afterward wine and fruit of which the peaches were excellent. At nine o'clock our host withdrew and everybody else as they pleased.

1822

A LETTER FROM AN EMIGRANT SON
by John Watson

BETWEEN 1820 AND 1860 more than five million emigrants left the Old World to try to make a home for themselves in the New World. The Industrial Revolution had robbed many workmen of their jobs in England and Europe. But America was a new and fast-growing country ready and eager to absorb laborers, farmers, shopkeepers and professional people of all kinds to man her factories, staff her young cities, and farm the virgin lands that were continually being opened up in the wake of her developing land and river transport.

John Watson was an English emigrant farmer. In a letter to his father he gives a factual account of the struggle he and his wife had to make a place for themselves and their children in America and of the success that crowned their struggle. The letter reveals two important factors that contributed to that success: an uncomplaining fortitude on the part of the emigrants and a warm and generous hospitality on the part of the Americans who, though poor themselves, were willing to give the strangers a helping hand because they knew from their own experience what it meant to be a pioneer in a new country.

Aurora, Dearborn County, Indiana State.
June 15, 1822

Dear Father,

Recollecting my promise to you not to write till I was perfectly settled, you would not expect a letter so soon as you might otherwise have done. I now consider myself as so settled.

You will recollect that I started with my wife and our children in the brig Wellington for St. John's, New Brunswick, where we arrived June 15th, 1819, after losing one of our mates by lightning and one seaman. There we remained till March 15, 1820. New Brunswick the winter too severe to profit much by farming. I determined to leave at all hazards. I therefore with my wife got a hand-sleigh, in which I placed the children, and drew them on the ice up the St. John's river about 360 miles, Mary and myself walking drawing the children after us. You must also recollect that 100 miles of this was not settled being all wood. We arrived at the head of St. John's river. We travelled on in the same manner across snow and ice to the great river St. Laurence, about 180 miles below Quebec; there we found the country along the bank thickly settled. I then built myself a light waggon, and had all our family provisioned during the time of making the waggon for "I thank you"; the good people who were French Canadians wishing us very much to stay with them. In this

64

waggon our children were drawn by myself for upwards of 400 miles to Kingston, at the mouth of Lake Ontario. There (as every other place, we met with uncommon kindness); a gentleman quite a stranger not only sent us by the steamboat free of all expense to Fort George, but put 6 or 7 dollars in our pockets besides. From Fort George we crossed into the United States, and passed the summer at Geneva, Ontario County, New York State.

Hearing a more favorable account of the State of Indiana, I once more started on a ramble, and travelling across the State of New York, I came to O'Lean Point in the Allegany river, which river, a very rapid one, I came down in a flat boat to Pittsburgh; here I stayed two days, and passing on, after being detained by head winds, and the water being very low, landed at Aurora, situated at the mouth of Hogan Creek.

Here I found myself a stranger without friends, acquaintance, utensils of any kind or *money,* having spent our last dollar a day or two before: added to which myself and all our family were caught by illness for 6 or 8 weeks, without the power of doing any thing. But no sooner was our situation known, then we had plenty of provisions brought to us, and as our strength recovered I obtained work at digging, etc. My wife took in sewing and by degrees we have worked it to that I have 2 cows, 2 calves, 9 pigs, and 1 calf expected in August.

James is now at school, and I intend to send two in the winter. I have joined with a farmer in cropping: that is I received one-half of the produce, and had the team found me. I am now working for an English gentleman named Harris, who is building in Aurora, and owns four quarter sections up the Creek. Much good land can be bought far distant for 1 dollar and a quarter per acre, and improved land for not much more; indeed, so good is the prospect for a man who must live by industry, that I wish all my friends and acquaintances were here with me. I can safely say, I would not, nor would my

Mary, return to England on any account whatsoever. We are now all in good health.

In the earnest desire of hearing from you,

I remain yours,

John Watson

The best port for you to come, would be Philadelphia or Baltimore.

To Mr. Stephen Watson
    Parish of Sedlescomb
    near Battle, Sussex, Old England

1827

ROCHESTER: A TOWN IN THE MAKING
by Captain Basil Hall

IN THE EARLY 19th century a fast-growing America was in urgent need of better and cheaper means of transport to promote trade and travel between the East and West and to bind the widely separated people into a unified nation.

In October 1825 the first great water road, the Erie Canal, was completed. It was 363 miles long and it had taken thousands of workmen eight long years to build. Running from Albany to Buffalo, it cut the cost of transport along its route from $100 to $10 a ton. The booming canal traffic benefited the whole district and especially the city of New York, which soon became the most important port in the United States. The Erie Canal also stimulated travel to the West and led to the development of cities like Cleveland, Detroit and Chicago. And all along the Canal farmers and tradesmen fought to buy land in such numbers that new cities seemed to grow up overnight.

Basil Hall, a former English naval officer, writer and tireless traveler, paid a visit to Rochester in 1827 when that city on the Erie Canal was a boom town, so new that not a single one of its 8,000 inhabitants had been born there.

The chief source of the commercial and agricultural prosperity of Rochester is the Erie Canal, as that village is made the emporium of the rich agricultural districts bordering on the Genesee river; and its capitalists both send out and import a vast quantity of wheat, flour, beef, pork, pot and pearl ashes, whiskey and so on. Out of more than 8,000 souls in this gigantic young village, there was not to be found in 1827 a single grown-up person born there, the oldest native not being then seventeen years of age.

On the 26th of June, 1827, we strolled through the village, under the guidance of a most obliging and intelligent friend, a native of this part of the country. Everything in this bustling place appeared to be in motion. The very streets seemed to be starting up of their own accord, ready-made, and looking as fresh and new, as if they had been turned out of the workmen's hands but an hour before, or that a great boxful of new houses had been sent by steam from New York, and tumbled out on the half-cleared land. The canal banks were at some places still unturfed; the lime seemed hardly dry in the masonry of the aqueduct, in the bridges, and in the numberless great saw-mills and manufactures. In many of these buildings the people were at work below stairs, while at top the carpenters were busy nailing on the planks of the roof.

Some dwellings were half painted, while the foundations of others, within five yards distance, were only beginning. I cannot say how many churches, court-houses, jails, and hotels I counted, all in motion, creeping upwards. Several streets were finished, but had as yet not received their names; and many others were in the reverse predicament, being named, but not commenced—their local habitation being merely signified by lines of stakes. Here and there we saw great warehouses, without window sashes, but half filled with goods, and furnished with hoisting cranes, ready to fish up the huge pyramids of flour barrels, bales, and boxes lying in the streets. In the centre of the town the spire of a Presbyterian church rose to a great height, and on each side of the supporting tower was to be seen the dial-plate of a clock, of which the machinery, in the hurry-scurry, had been left at New York. I need not say that these half-finished, whole-finished, and embryo streets were crowded with people, carts, stages, cattle, pigs, far beyond the reach of numbers;—and as all these were lifting up their voices together, in keeping with the clatter of hammers, the ringing of axes, and the creaking of machinery, there was a fine concert, I assure you!

A few years ago the whole of that part of the country was covered with a dark silent forest, and even as it was, we could not proceed a mile in any direction except that of the high-road, without coming full-butt against the woods of time immemorial. When land is cleared for the purposes of cultivation, the stumps are left standing for many years, from its being easier, as well as more profitable in other respects, to plough round them, than to waste time and labour in rooting them out, or burning them, or blowing them up with gunpowder. But when a forest is levelled with a view to building a town in its place, a different system must of course be adopted. The trees must be removed sooner or later, according to the means of the proprietor or the necessities of the case. Thus one man possessed of capital will clear his lot of the wood, and erect houses, or even streets, across it; while on his neighbor's land the trees may still be growing. And it actually occurred to us, several times, within the immediate limits of the inhabited town itself, in streets, too, where shops were opened, and all sorts of business actually going on, that we had to drive first on one side, and then on the other, to avoid the stumps of an oak, or a hemlock, or a pine tree, staring us full in the face.

After we had gone about a mile from town the forest thickened, we lost sight of every trace of a human dwelling, or of human inter-ference with nature in any shape. We stood considering what we should do next, when the loud crash of a falling tree met our ears. Our friendly guide was quite glad, he said, to have this opportunity of exhibiting the very first step in the process of town-making. After a zig-zag scramble amongst trees, which had been allowed to grow up and decay century after century, we came to a spot where three or four men were employed in clearing out a street, as they declared, though any thing more unlike a street could not well be conceived. Nevertheless, the ground in question certainly formed part of the plan of the town. It had been chalked out by surveyors' stakes, and some speculators having taken up the lots for immediate building, of course found it necessary to open a street through the woods, to afford a line of communication with the rest of the village. As fast as the trees were cut down, they were stripped of their branches and drawn off by oxen, sawed into planks, or otherwise fashioned to the purpose of building without delay. There was little or no exaggeration, there-fore, in supposing with our friend, that the same fir which might be waving about in full life and vigor in the morning, should be cut down, dragged into daylight, squared, framed, and before night, be hoisted up to make a beam or rafter to some tavern, or factory, or store, at the corner of a street, which twenty-four hours before had existed only on paper, and yet might be completed, from end to end, within a week afterwards.

A SLAVE VILLAGE
by Captain Basil Hall

IN READING THE ACCOUNT of a slave village by Captain Basil Hall, it must be borne in mind that while he was an honest and skillful observer, he was also a High Tory. His sympathies were with the slave owners rather than with the slaves, and his cosy picture of "shining urchins" and "comfortable cottages" may therefore have been to some extent due to rose-colored glasses.

It appears that when the negroes go to the field in the morning, it is the custom to leave such children behind, as are too young to work. Accordingly, we found a sober old matron in charge of three dozen shining urchins, collected together in a house near the centre of the village. Over the fire hung a large pot of hominy, a preparation of Indian corn, making ready for the little folks' supper, and a very merry, happy-looking party they seemed. The parents, and such children as are old enough to be useful, go out to work at daybreak, taking their dinner with them to eat on the ground.

We went into several of the cottages, which were uncommonly neat and comfortable and might have shamed those of many countries I have seen. Each hut was divided into small rooms or compartments, fitted with regular bed-places; besides which, they had all chimneys and doors, and some, though only a few of them, possessed the luxury of windows. I counted twenty-eight huts, occupied by one hundred and forty souls, or about five in each. This number included sixty children.

LIFE IN CINCINNATI
by Frances Trollope

FRANCES TROLLOPE, the mother of the famous novelist Anthony Trollope, came to America in 1827 with two daughters and a son to see if she could recoup the sagging family fortunes by opening a store in Cincinnati. The store turned out to be a failure, a fact which did little to endear the crude little midwestern city to the sophisticated, fastidious and sharp-tongued Mrs. Trollope. By 1831 she was safely home in England again where she published *Domestic Manners of the Americans,* a book about her life in America, which was consistently witty but not always polite. Greeted with amusement in England and with rage in the United States, it was a best seller on both sides of the Atlantic.

We reached Cincinnati on the 10th of February. It is finely situated on the south side of a hill that rises gently from the water's edge; yet it is by no means a city of striking appearance: it wants domes, towers, and steeples; but its landing-place is noble, extending for more than a quarter of a mile; it is well paved, and surrounded by neat, though not handsome buildings. I have seen fifteen steam-boats lying there at once, and still half the wharf was unoccupied.

We were soon settled in our new dwelling, which looked neat and comfortable enough, but we speedily found that it was devoid of nearly all the accommodation that Europeans conceive necessary to decency and comfort. No pump, no cistern, no drain of any kind, no dustman's cart, or any other visible means of getting rid of the rubbish, which vanishes with such celerity in London, that one has no time to think of its existence; but which accumulated so rapidly at Cincinnati, that I sent for my landlord to know in what manner refuse of all kinds was to be disposed of.

"Your Help will just have to fix them all into the middle of the street, but you must mind, old woman, that it is the middle. I expect you don't know as we have got a law what forbids throwing such things at the sides of the streets; they must just all be cast right into the middle, and the pigs soon takes them off."

In truth the pigs are constantly doing Herculean service in this way through every quarter of the city; and though it is not very agreeable to live surrounded by herds of these unsavoury animals, it is well they are so numerous and so active in their capacity of scavengers, for without them the streets would soon be choked up with all sorts of substances in every stage of decomposition.

The greatest difficulty in organising a family establishment in Ohio, is getting servants, or, as it is there called "getting help," for it is more than petty treason to the Republic, to call a free citizen a *servant*. A kind friend, however, exerted herself so effectually for me, that a tall, stately lass soon presented herself, saying, "I be come to help you." The intelligence was very agreeable, and I welcomed her in the most gracious manner possible, and asked what I could give her by the year.

"Oh Gimini!" exclaimed the damsel, with a loud laugh, "You be a downright Englisher, sure enough. I should like to see a young lady engage by the year in America! I hope I shall get a husband before many months, or I expect I shall be an outright old maid, for I be most seventeen already; besides, mayhap I may want to go to school. You must just give me a dollar and a half a week, and mother's slave, Phillis, must come over once a week, I expect, from t'other side of the water to help me clean."

I agreed to the bargain, of course, with all dutiful submission; and seeing she was preparing to set to work in a yellow dress parsemé with red roses, I gently hinted, that I thought it was a pity to spoil so fine a gown, and that she had better change it.

72

" 'Tis just my best and my worst," she answered, "for I've got no other."

I immediately gave her money to purchase what was necessary for cleanliness and decency, and set to work with my daughters to make her a gown. She grinned applause when our labour was completed, but never uttered the slightest expression of gratitude for that, or for anything else we could do for her. She was constantly asking us to lend her different articles of dress, and when we declined it, she said, "Well I never seed such grumpy folks as you be; there is several young ladies of my acquaintance what goes to live out now and then with the old women about town, and they and their gurls always lends them what they ask for."

This young lady left me at the end of two months, because I refused to lend her money enough to buy a silk dress to go to a ball, saying, "Then 'tis not worth my while to stay any longer."

From the want of pasturage near the city, it is difficult for a stranger to divine how milk is furnished for its supply, but we soon learnt that there are more ways than one of keeping a cow. A large proportion of the families in the town, particularly of the poorer class, have one, though apparently without any accommodation whatever for it. These animals are fed morning and evening at the door of the house, with a good mess of Indian corn, boiled with water; while they eat, they are milked, and when the operation is completed the milk-pail and the meal-tub retreat into the dwelling, leaving the republican cow to walk away, to take her pleasure on the hills, or in the gutters, as may suit her fancy best. They generally return very regularly to give and take the evening meal; though it more than once happened to us to have our jug sent home empty, with the sad news that "the cow was not come home, and it was too late to look for her to breakfast now." Once, I remember, the good woman told us that she had overslept herself, and that the cow had come home and gone again, "not liking, I expect, to hanker about by herself for nothing, poor thing."

I never saw any people who appeared to live so much without amusement as the Cincinnatians. Billiards are forbidden by law, so are cards. They have no public balls, excepting, I think, six, during the Christmas holidays. They have no concerts. They have no dinner parties.

They have a theatre, which is, in fact, the only public amusement of this triste little town; but they seem to care little about it, and either from economy or distaste, it is very poorly attended. Ladies are rarely seen there, and by far the larger proportion of females deem it an offense against religion to witness the representation of a play. It is in the churches and chapels of the town that the ladies are to be seen in full costume; and I am tempted to believe that a stranger from the continent of Europe would be inclined, on first reconnoitering the city, to suppose that the places of worship were the theatres and cafes of the place.

1831—1832

THE PIONEER
by Alexis de Tocqueville

IN 1831 THE FRENCH government sent one of its assistant magistrates to America to study prisons and penitentiaries there. His name was Alexis Charles Henri Maurice Clerel de Tocqueville. Keenly observant and admirably open-minded, Tocqueville during his stay in the United States saw a great deal more than the prison system he had come to investigate. Neither pro- nor anti-democracy, he looked at the American democratic government with a dispassionate eye and, on his return home, wrote a book, *De la Démocratie en Amérique (Democracy in America)*, which not only was highly successful in his own day, but has since become a classic.

In the account of the pioneer that follows, Tocqueville shows the brilliance of mind and the writing talent which have made him famous.

The bells which the pioneer is careful to hang round his beasts' necks so as to find them again in the dense forest, give warning in the far distance that one is getting near to a clearing. Soon one hears the echoes of the axe that is cutting down the forest trees, and as one gets closer, signs of destruction make man's presence ever more evident. Severed branches cover the road, and trunks half scorched by fire or cut about by the axe, yet stand still erect in your path. As you go on your way, you come to a wood where all the trees seem to have been struck by sudden death. In full summer their withered branches seem the image of winter. Looking at them close-up, you see that a deep circle has been cut in their bark, which, by preventing the circulation of the sap, has brought them to a speedy death. That, in fact, is usually the planter's first beginning. As he cannot, in the first year, cut all the trees that adorn his new property, he sows corn under their branches and, by striking them to death, prevents them from shading his crop. After this field which is an unfinished sketch, a first step of civilisation in the wilds, one suddenly sees the owner's cabin. It is generally placed in the middle of some land more carefully cultivated than the rest, but where man is yet sustaining an unequal fight against nature. There the trees had been cut but not grubbed up: their trunks still cover and block the land they used to shade. Round this withered debris, wheat, shoots of oak, plants of all kinds, and weeds of all sorts are scattered pell-mell and grow up together in the untamed and still half-wild ground. It is in the middle of this vigorous and variegated growth of vegetation that the planter's dwelling or, as it is called in this country, his log-house rises. Just like the field around it, this rustic dwelling shows every sign of new and hurried work. It is seldom more than 30 feet long. It is 20 feet wide and 15 high. Both its walls and its roof are made of unsquared tree-trunks between which moss and earth have been rammed to keep the cold and rain out from the inside of the house. The closer the traveller gets, the more animated the scene becomes. As they hear his footsteps, the children playing in the surrounding debris, get up in a hurry and run for shelter to their father's house, as if they were frightened at the sight of a man, while two great half-wild dogs with ears pricked and long muzzles, come out of the cabin and growling cover their young masters' retreat.

It is then that the pioneer himself appears at the door of his dwelling; he takes a good look at the new arrival; signs to his dogs to go back under cover and himself hastens to give them the example without a sign of curiosity or anxiety.

When he gets to the threshold of the log-house, the European cannot help casting an astonished glance round the sight before him.

Such a cabin generally has but one window, at which perhaps a muslin curtain is hanging; for in these parts where necessities are not seldom lacking, superfluities often abound. A resinous fire crackles on the hearth of beaten earth, and, better than the daylight, lights up the inside of the place. Over this rustic fire one sees trophies of war or hunt: a long rifle, a deerskin, some eagle's feathers. To the right of the chimney a map of the United States is often stretched and the draught that blows through the gaps in the wall keeps raising and fluttering it. By it on a single shelf of ill-squared planks are a few tattered books; there one finds a Bible with its cloth and boards already worn out by the piety of two generations, a prayer-book and, sometimes, a poem of Milton or a tragedy of Shakespeare. Along the wall are some rough seats, made by the hands of the owner himself; some trunks instead of cupboards, some agricultural implements and samples of the harvest. In the middle of the room is a rickety table whose legs, still sprouting foliage, seem to have grown by themselves on the ground they cover. It is there that the whole family assembles every day to take their meals. One also sees an English china teapot, some spoons usually of wood, some cracked cups and newspapers.

The looks of the master of this dwelling are no less remarkable than the place that gives them shelter.

His angular muscles and thin limbs make one recognise at first glance the inhabitant of New England. This man has not been born to the solitude where he lives. His temperament alone makes that clear. His first years were passed in a society used to thought and argument. It is the strength of his will that has taken him to do work in the wilds to which he seems so little adapted. But if his physical powers seem too slight for this undertaking, his features lined by the cares of life bespeak a practical intelligence, and a cold, persevering energy that strike one at first sight. His movements are slow and stiff, his words measured and his appearance austere. Habit and still more pride have given his features that Stoic stiffness that his deeds belie: it is true that the pioneer scorns things that often move mens' hearts most violently; his goods and life will never depend on the chance of a throw of dice, or the fate of a woman; but to win affluence he has braved exile, the solitude and innumerable wretchednesses of life in the wilds, he has slept on the bare ground and risked fever in the forest and the Indian tomahawk. He has one day made that effort, and renewed it through the years; perhaps he will carry on with it for twenty years more without discouragement or complaint. Can a man capable of such sacrifices be a cold, unfeeling being? Should one not rather recognise that he is consumed by some burning, tenacious, implacable passion of the mind?

In speaking of the pioneer one cannot forget the companion of his trials and dangers. Look at that young woman at the other side of the hearth who as she sees to cooking the meal rocks her youngest son on her knees. Like the emigrant this woman is in the flower of her

77

age; like him, she can remember the affluence of her first years. Her dress still shows an ill-suppressed taste for clothes but time has pressed heavily on her. By her features worn before their time, by her wasted limbs it is easy to see that existence has been a heavy burden for her. The pioneer's wife, carried off in an instant and without hope of return from her innocent cradle of youth, has exchanged the charms of society and the joys of the domestic hearth for the solitude of the forest. To devote herself to austere duties, to submit to privations once unknown to her, to embrace an existence for which she was not made, such has been the work of the best years of her life, such for her have been the delights of conjugal union. Want, suffering and boredom have changed her fragile frame but not broken down her courage. Amid the deep sadness engraved on her delicate features it is easy to see something of religious resignation, a profound peace and I cannot say what natural firmness and tranquility that faces all the trials of life without fear or boast.

Half-naked children bursting with health, thoughtless of the morrow, true sons of the wild, press round this woman. Their mother looks from time to time at them half in sadness, half in joy. To see their strength and her weakness one would say that she has drained herself to give them life and does not regret what they have cost her.

The dwelling in which the emigrants live has no internal division and no storehouse. The whole family comes to seek shelter of an evening in the single room which it contains. This dwelling forms as it were a little world of its own. It is an ark of civilization lost in the midst of an ocean of leaves, it is a sort of oasis in the desert. A hundred paces beyond it the everlasting forest stretches its shades around it and solitude begins again.

1835

TRAVEL IN SOUTH CAROLINA
by Harriet Martineau

HARRIET MARTINEAU was an English writer whose life began with many handicaps. Delicate from birth, lacking a sense of taste and smell, and hard of hearing besides, she lost her brother, her father and her fiancé in rapid succession. A short time later she lost all her money in a business failure. At first she was forced to support herself by taking in sewing; but, discovering that she had a talent for writing, she worked hard and courageously until she became a prolific and popular author.

In 1834 Harriet Martineau decided to go to America to see for herself what life was like in the new and vigorous country everyone was talking about. In spite of her poor health she stayed two years, traveling indefatigably, and on returning home she wrote two books about her experiences which were widely read: *Society in America* and *A Retrospect of Western Travel*.

The traffic on these roads is so small, that the stranger feels himself almost lost in the wilderness. In the course of several days' journey, we saw (with the exception of the wagons of a few encampments) only one vehicle besides our own. It was a stage returning from Charleston. Our meeting in the forest was like the meeting of ships at sea. We asked the passengers from the south for news of Charleston and Europe, they questioned us about the state of politics at Washington.

An account of an actual day's journey will give the best idea of what travelling is in such places. We had travelled from Richmond, Virginia, the day before [March 2nd, 1835], and had not had any rest, when, at midnight, we came to a river which had no bridge. The "scow" had gone over with another stage, and we stood under the stars for a long time: hardly less than an hour. The scow was only just large enough to hold the coach and ourselves; so that it was thought safest for passengers to alight, and go on board on foot. In this process I found myself over the ankles in mud. A few minutes after we had driven on again, on the opposite side of the river, we had to get out to change coaches; after which we proceeded, without accident, though very slowly till daylight. Then the coach sank down in a deep rut, and the horses struggled in vain. We were informed that we were "mired," and we must all get out. I stood for some time to witness what is very pretty for once; but wearisome when it occurs ten times a day. The driver carries an axe, as a part of the stage apparatus. He cuts down a young tree for a lever, which is introduced under the nave of the sunken wheel; a log serving for a block. The gentlemen passengers all help; shouting to the horses, which tug and scramble as vigorously as the gentlemen. We ladies sometimes gave our humble assistance by blowing the driver's horn. Sometimes a cluster of negroes would assemble from a neighboring plantation; and in extreme cases, they would bring a horse, to add to our team. The rescue from the rut was effected in any time from a quarter of an hour to two hours. This particular third of March, two hours were lost by this first mishap. It was very cold, and I walked on alone, sure of not missing my road in a region where there was no other. When I had proceeded two miles, I stopped and looked around me. I was on a rising ground, with no object whatever visible but the wild, black forest, extending on all sides as far as I could see, and the red road cut through it, straight as an arrow, till it was lost behind a rising ground at either extremity. The stage soon after took me up, and we proceeded fourteen miles to breakfast. We were faint with hunger; but there was no refreshment for us. The family breakfast had been long over, and there was not a scrap of food in the house. We proceeded, till at one o'clock we reached a private dwelling, where the good woman was kind enough to provide dinner for us, though the family had dined. She gave us a comfortable meal, and charged only a quarter dollar each.

We had no sooner left her house than we had to get out to pass on foot a bridge too crazy for us to venture over it in the carriage. Half a mile before reaching the place where we were to have tea, the thorough-brace broke, and we had to walk through a snow shower to the inn. We had not proceeded above a quarter of a mile from this place when the traces broke. After this, we were allowed to sit still in the carriage till nearly seven in the morning, when we were approaching Raleigh, North Carolina. We then saw a carriage "mired" and deserted by driver and horses but tenanted by some travellers who had been waiting these since eight the evening before. While we were pitying their fate, our vehicle once more sank into a rut. It was, however, extricated in a short time, and we reached Raleigh in safety.

It was worth undergoing a few travelling disasters to witness the skill and temper of the drivers, and the inexhaustible good-nature of the passengers. Men of business in any other part of the world would be visibly annoyed by such delays as I have described; but in America I never saw any gentleman's temper give way under these accidents. Every one jumps out in a moment, and sets to work to help the driver; every one has his joke, and, when it is over, the ladies are sure to have the whole represented to them in its most amusing light.

1836

THE LAND BOOM: CHICAGO
by Harriet Martineau

In the summer of 1836, the delicate but tireless Harriet Martineau was still busily investigating America. With a party of friends she traveled to Chicago where she was both astonished and fascinated by the crude but powerful life of the young American West.

I never saw a busier place than Chicago was at the time of our arrival. The streets were crowded with land speculators, hurrying from one sale to another. A negro, dressed up in scarlet, bearing a scarlet flag, and riding a white horse with housings of scarlet, announced the times of sale. At every street-corner where he stopped, the crowd flocked round him; and it seemed as if some prevalent mania infected the whole people. As the gentlemen of our party walked the streets, store-keepers hailed them from their doors, with offers of farms, and all manner of land-lots, advising them to speculate before the price of land rose higher. A young lawyer of my acquaintance there, had realised five hundred dollars per day, the five preceding days, by merely taking out titles to land. Another friend had realised, in two years, ten times as much money as he had before fixed upon as a competence for life. Of course this rapid making of money is a merely temporary evil. A bursting of the bubble must come soon.

The immediate occasion of the bustle which prevailed the week we were in Chicago, was the sale of lots, in the value of two million dollars, along the course of a projected canal; and of another set immediately behind these. Persons not intending to game and not infected with mania, would endeavor to form some reasonable conjecture as to the ultimate value of the lots, by calculating the cost of the canal, the risks from accident, from the possible competition from other places, etc., and, finally the possible profits, under the most favorable circumstances, within so many years' purchase. Such a calculation would serve as some sort of guide as to the amount of purchase money to be risked. Whereas wild land on the banks of a canal, not yet even marked out, was selling at Chicago for more than rich land, well improved, in the finest part of the valley of the Mohawk, on the banks of a canal which is already the medium of an almost inestimable amount of traffic.

Others, besides lawyers and speculators by trade, make a fortune in such extraordinary times. A poor man at Chicago had a preemption right to some land, for which he paid in the morning one hundred and fifty dollars. In the afternoon he sold it to a friend of mine for five thousand dollars. A poor Frenchman, married to a squaw, had a suit pending, when I was there, which he was likely to gain, for the right of purchasing some land by the lake for one hundred dollars, which would immediately become worth one million dollars.

When the present intoxication of prosperity passes away, some of the inhabitants will go back to the eastward; there will be an accession of settlers from the mechanic classes; good houses will have been built for the richer families, and the singularity of the place will subside. It will be like all the other new and thriving lake and river ports of America. Meantime, I am glad to have seen it in its strange early days.

1842

BY CANAL BOAT TO PITTSBURGH
by Charles Dickens

IN 1842 CHARLES DICKENS came to the United States on a combination lecture and sight-seeing tour. His fame as a novelist was already world-wide, and the American public welcomed the visiting literary lion with a warmth that bordered on hysteria. The over-effusive welcome, with its demands on his time and energies, exhausted the writer and combined with the unjust copyright laws of the time (Americans were allowed to pirate the Dickens works) to give him a distaste for the United States. On his return to England, Dickens set to work on *Martin Chuzzlewit* and incorporated into this novel some bitter criticism of America and the Americans.

As a result public opinion in the United States cooled toward Charles Dickens, the man; but the popularity of Dickens, the writer, never wavered.

I remained in a vague state of mind until ten o'clock or thereabouts, when going below, I found suspended on either side of the cabin, three long tiers of hanging book-shelves, designed apparently for volumes of the small octavo size. Looking with greater attention at these contrivances (wondering to find such literary preparations in such a place), I descried on each shelf a sort of microscopic sheet and blanket; then I began dimly to comprehend that the passengers were the library, and that they were to be arranged, edge-wise, on these shelves, till morning.

The politeness of the person in authority had secured to me a shelf in a nook, in some degree removed from the great body of sleepers: to which place I retired, with many acknowledgements to him for his attention. I found it, on after-measurement, just the width of an ordinary sheet of Bath post letter-paper; and I was at first in some uncertainty as to the best means of getting into it. But the shelf being a bottom one, I finally determined on lying upon the floor, roll-ing gently in, stopping immediately I touched the mattress, and re-maining for the night with that side uppermost, whatever it might be. Luckily, I came upon my back at exactly the right moment. I was much alarmed on looking upward, to see, by the shape of his half-yard of sacking (which his weight had bent into an exceedingly tight bag), that there was a very heavy gentleman above me, whom the slender cords seemed quite incapable of holding; and I could not help reflecting upon the grief of my wife and family in the event of his coming down in the night.

All night long, and every night on this canal, there was a perfect storm of spitting; and once my coat, being in the very centre of the hurricane sustained by five gentlemen, I was fain the next morning to lay it on the deck and rub it down with fair water before it was in a condition to be worn again.

Between five and six o'clock in the morning we got up, and some of us went on deck to give them an opportunity of taking the shelves down. The washing accommodations were primitive. There was a tin ladle chained to the deck, with which every gentleman who thought it necessary to cleanse himself (many were superior to this weakness), fished the dirty water out of the canal, and poured it into a tin basin, secured in like manner. There was also a jack-towel. And, hanging up before a little looking-glass in the bar, in the immediate vicinity of the bread and cheese and biscuits, were a public comb and hair-brush.

At eight o'clock, the shelves being taken down and put away and the table joined together, everybody sat down to the tea, coffee, bread, butter, salmon, shad, liver, steak, potatoes, pickles, ham, chops, black-puddings, and sausages. When everybody had done with everything, the fragments were cleared away: and one of the waiters appearing anew in the character of a barber, shaved such of the company as desired to be shaved; while the remainder looked on, or yawned over their newspapers. Dinner was breakfast again, without the tea and coffee; and supper and breakfast were identical.

And yet, despite the oddities—there was much in this mode of travelling which I heartily enjoyed at the time, and look back upon with great pleasure.

1846

From A SECOND VISIT TO THE UNITED STATES
by Sir Charles Lyell

SIR CHARLES LYELL was a distinguished British scientist, President of the Geological Society of London. He paid two visits to the United States, one in 1841, the other in 1845–46. Although Lyell was interested first of all in the geology of America, his intelligent interest in everything he saw and his trained scientific mind made him a perceptive traveler and a just reporter of the life that went on around him.

The banks of the Alabama, like those of the Savannah and Altamaha rivers, are fringed with canes, over which usually towers the deciduous cypress, covered with pendent moss. Some of the largest trees on the banks are sycamores, called button-wood, one of which I measured, and found it to be eighteen feet in circumference. The old bark is continually peeling off, and the new is as white as if the trunk had been painted.

When it was growing dusk, and nearly all had retired to their cabins, and some to their beds, we were startled by a loud crash, as if parts of the wood-work of the steamer were giving way over our heads. At the same moment a shower of broken glass came rattling down on the floor of the cabin. As I expected to land in the course of the night at Claiborne, I had not taken off my clothes, so I rushed immediately on deck. Crash after crash of broken spars and the ringing of shattered window-glasses were still heard, and the confusion and noise were indescribable. "Don't be alarmed; we have only got among the trees," said the captain. This, I found, was no uncommon occurrence when these enormous vessels are sweeping down at full speed in the flood season. In this predicament I found the *Amaranth* when I got on deck. Many a strong bough had pierced through the cabin windows on one side, throwing down the lights, and smashing the wooden balustrade and the roof of the long gallery, and tearing the canvas awning from the verandah. The engine had been backed, or its motion reversed, but the steamer, held fast by the trees, was swinging round with the force of the current. A large body of men were plying their axes freely, not only cutting off the boughs, but treating with no respect the framework of the cabin itself. I could not help feeling thankful that no branch had obtruded itself into our berths. At length we got off, and the carpenters and glaziers set to work immediately to make repairs.

In the course of the night we were informed that the *Amaranth* had reached Claiborne. Here we found a flight of wooden steps, like a ladder, leading up the nearly perpendicular bluff which was 150 feet high. By the side of these steps was a framework of wood, forming the inclined plane down which the cotton bales were lowered by ropes. Captain Bragdon politely gave his arm to my wife, and two negroes preceded us with blazing torches of pine-wood, throwing their light on the bright, shining leaves of several splendid magnolias. We were followed by a long train of negroes each carrying some article of our baggage. Having ascended the steps, we came to a flat terrace, covered with grass, the first green sward we had seen for many weeks, and found there a small, quiet inn, where we resolved to spend some days, to make a collection of the fossil tertiary shells, so well known to geologists as abounding in the strata of this cliff.

1846

AMERICAN LIFE
by Louis Agassiz

LOUIS AGASSIZ, a well-known Swiss man of science, came to the United States in 1846 on a grant from the King of Prussia. He had two main objectives: to study the natural history and geology of the country and to give a series of lectures, which had been arranged for him by Sir Charles Lyell, at the Lowell Institute in Boston. A brilliant scientist and a magnetic speaker, Louis Agassiz was an immediate success with his American audiences; and the new, young, democratic country was an equal success with the visiting scientist, who decided to make his permanent home in the United States.

In 1848 Harvard appointed Agassiz Professor of Natural History, a post he occupied until his death in 1873. His second wife, Elizabeth Carey Agassiz, was the founder of Radcliffe College and served as its president for a number of years.

In a letter to his mother, written soon after his arrival in the United States, Agassiz gives some of his first impressions of America.

A characteristic feature of American life is to be found in the frequent public meetings where addresses are delivered. Shortly after my arrival in Boston, I was present at a meeting of some three thousand workmen, foremen of workshops, clerks, and the like. No meeting could have been more respectable and well-conducted. All were neatly dressed; even the simplest laborer had a clean shirt. It was a strange sight to see such an assemblage, brought together for the purpose of forming a library, and listening attentively in perfect quiet for two hours to an address on the advantages of education, of reading, and the means of employing usefully the leisure moments of a workman's life. The most eminent men vie with each other in instructing and forming the education of the population at large. I have not yet seen a man out of employment or a beggar, except in New

York, which is a sink for the emptying of Europe. Yet do not think that I forget the advantages of our old civilization. Far from it. I feel more than ever the value of a past which belongs to you and in which you have grown up. Generations must pass before America will have the collections of art and science which adorn our cities, or the establishments for public instruction, sanctuaries as it were, consecrated by the devotion of those who give themselves wholly to study. Here all the world works to gain a livelihood or to make a fortune. Few establishments [universities] are old enough to have taken sufficiently deep roots in the habits of the people, to be safe from innovation: very few institutions offer a combination of studies, such as, in its ensemble, meets the demands of modern civilization. All is done by the single efforts of individuals or of corporations, too often guided by the needs of the moment. This American science lacks the scope which is characteristic of higher instruction in Europe. Objects of art are curiosities but little appreciated and usually still less understood. On the other hand the whole population shares in the advanced education provided for all.

1847

A FRONTIER TRADING POST
From the Journal of Rudolph Friederich Kurz

RUDOLPH FRIEDERICH KURZ was a Swiss artist who came to America because, as he puts it, "From my earliest youth primeval forest and Indians had an indescribable charm for me. From the moment I determined to become an artist, my life purpose was fixed: I would devote my talents to the portrayal of the aboriginal forests, the wild animals that inhabited them, and to the Indians."

He spent the winter of 1847 at St. Joseph, a typical frontier post on the Missouri River. There were plenty of Indians and plenty of primeval forest at St. Joseph, for the region in the midst of which the town was situated was open Indian country, belonging to the Kickapoo tribe. The frontier post itself was a meeting place for all the fur traders of Missouri and Nebraska.

St. Joseph, once the trading post of Joseph Robidoux, is situated at the foot of the Black Snake Hills on the left bank of the Missouri. Though the town was founded only six years ago, there are evidences already of a rapidly expanding and flourishing city. In spite of the fact that there are many new buildings, both of wood and brick, houses, either for homes or for business purposes, are hard to get. Upon my arrival, the principal streets were much enlivened by the fur traders and immigrants on their way to regions, as yet little known, in Oregon and California. The rich gold mines were not then discovered. Only the most daring fur traders had penetrated into that far country and, following in their wake, a rough, lawless set of adventurers, eager for gain and best pleased with what the strong hand won, traveled the same trail in armed bands with pack mules and covered wagons.

Indians of various tribes—the Potawatomi, the Foxes (Musquakee), Kickapoo, Iowa, and Oto—one sees constantly in this town, particularly at the landing where they take the ferry-boat to cross the river. They conduct themselves in a very dignified manner. Now and then, to be sure, when one of them has drunk too much of the forbidden whiskey, he is somewhat quarrelsome, but no more than an intoxicated white man.

Throughout the entire summer, bourgeois or the heads of firms, clerks, and other engagees or employees of the different fur companies, crowded the streets and public houses of the town. St. Joseph is for them now what St. Louis was earlier—their rendezvous. Here all style commodities are supplied from St. Louis, but horses are brought up for the purpose of selling them to the Indians on the upper Missouri and on the Platte or Nebraska. There, packs of buffalo hides (as many as ten packs at a time) are reshipped on the steamers, the empty mackinaw boats sold and their crews discharged. Those people are called Mountaineers. The Mountaineers like best to dress themselves in clothes made of tanned deerskin, embroidered and fringed. They are stared at as though they were bears.

My intercourse with these Mountaineers was very pleasant. Those with whom I talked were half-breeds who gave me much information and taught me, besides, the Indian language of signs. This knowledge of the sign language was of the utmost importance to me, even in St. Joseph, for I came in contact there with Indians from so many different tribes that I was at first hopelessly confused by their various dialects.

One of my hobbies was to collect Indian weapons, decorations and apparel. Before I learned the sign for "swap," I rarely succeeded in making a purchase unless I had an interpreter. The reason was that, in my bungling manner, I had made the sign "give." When a man presses the desired object to his breast and gives the Indian a questioning look, he is requesting a gift; when he points out the article he wishes, then strikes his right forefinger twice across his left forefinger, he means barter or trade. I soon became better acquainted with the Indians, when I was able by means of signs to purchase moccasins, bows and arrows, tobacco pipes, embroidered purses, bracelets, and clothing.

In the late autumn of 1848 the Missouri froze over to such a depth that a four horse team of sleighs laden with wood could cross without the slightest danger. This ice-bound passageway gave to many Americans easy access to the Indian forests, where they collected enormous amounts of firewood and took it away without compensation to the owners and sold it to the city. Finally the chief of the Kickapoo complained to the United States land agents, who then had a prohibitory order issued.

Near the end of the year 1848 about 30 lodges of Iowa Indians camped in the forest across the river from St. Joseph.

They came to get the benefit of clippings and cuttings of meat and the wastage incident upon the hog-killing season. Since they must live by hunting, the winter is a difficult time for the Indians, and particularly grave in those forests where wild animals are well-nigh exterminated. The buffalo and the elk have retreated long since to regions farther west. Following the chase under such conditions, in the frosts and mists, over ground covered with snow and ice, is extremely hard.

The chief of the band or kindred tribe of 30 Iowa families, or lodges, was called Kirutsche. As soon as Kirutsche was encamped and the entire settlement in order, he came to invite me to a dance that was to be given in his honor the next evening by some of his friends. I accepted the invitation with delight.

It was the evening of December 15. As I was crossing the frozen stream, an ice-cold wind swept across the river, driving before it a cloud of snowflakes.

In the forest I found some converging paths and did not know which one would lead to Kirutsche's tent. As soon, however, as I was well into the wood, out of the howling wind, I heard the measured beating of a drum. Following in the direction of that sound, I arrived in a short time at the lodge. I had expected to find a tent of skins similar to those I had already passed, but this was a hut constructed of withes in elliptical form and over-arched with rush mats. At the top there was an opening for light and for the egress of smoke and, cut low in one of the long side walls, was another that served for a door. The latter was covered, as by a curtain, with an animal pelt.

When I wished to go through the narrow door, I found a great tall Indian stationed there as guard. He was unwilling to let me in.

Kirutsche's squaw, who had already seen me, called to her husband, however, and he came at once to greet me. Kirutsche bid me sit down beside his beautiful daughter, Witthae. We could exchange very few words to be sure; we had to converse, therefore, by means of signs and eyes. To express my good will, I presented some small gifts that I had taken along with me for that purpose. It was then that I learned what I often put to the test later on: that one becomes acquainted with Indians much more quickly if one does not understand their speech.

My beautiful neighbor did not absorb all of my attention, however, to the exclusion of the dance. Around a large fire that was burning in the centre of the lodge sat twenty men and young blades. At the upper end Kirutsche sat on the floor, just as all Indians sit, with his legs crooked under him. Beside him were grouped his special friends and two drummers who, to the measured drum-beats, sang loud a repetition of "Oh!"

Two young men leaped, one behind the other, around the open space between the fire and the onlookers; each of them holding back the blanket with his left hand, carried in his right a slender whistle made of bone with which, inclining now to the ground, now toward the heavens, then toward the fire, then toward the guests, he blew a succession of harsh tuneless sounds. Then, varying the movements, the two performers went slowly round the circle and addressed themselves to each of the older guests. With the right hand they indicated the person to whom they would speak, said something flattering, whereupon the latter would reply "Hau" or "Hun" (abbreviations for "yes"). After they had spoken to every one in the circle and had repeated the bounding and whistling act, the two young men and the drummers were relieved from further duty. However, before the new performers came into action, whiskey was served in a wooden cup, to inspirit the guests.

To avoid accidents, in case of inebriation, Witthae collected all the knives (no Indian, man or woman, ever fails to carry a knife at the belt) and hid them.

In about three hours the whiskey flagon was empty, the people were tired, and the guests began to disperse. As finale, an old witch of a woman who had become intoxicated, gave a solo dance. With her long hair wildly disheveled, she stood with back bent and elbows akimbo, moving her arms alternately backward and forward, while with her feet close together she hopped, now to the right, now to the left, keeping time to the measured drum-beats and her own outcry.

Then I had to search my way home through the forest. I wrapped my riding cloak close about me and stamped cautiously along in the direction of the river, sometimes climbing over a fallen tree, sometimes wading knee-deep in a snowdrift, but exulting all the way over at the thought of having spent an evening in a lodge.

1850

PEOPLE
by Fredrika Bremer

FREDRIKA BREMER was a well-known Swedish novelist. Armed with letters of introduction, she traveled to America in 1849. There she met all the great American literary figures and established with them a cordial intimacy. She was middle-aged, frail and highly intelligent, and Nathaniel Hawthorne called her, "the funniest little fairy person one could imagine . . . a withered, briar rose, still reflecting the freshness of morning." In letters to her sister in Sweden she gave her opinions on everything she saw and drew candid portraits of her American hosts.

Washington Irving

There was a whole crowd of strangers to dinner at Mr. Hamilton's, among whom was Washington Irving, a man of about sixty, with large, beautiful eyes, a large, well-formed nose, a face still handsome, in which youthful little dimples and smiles bear witness to a youthfully fresh and humorous disposition and soul. He is also said to have an unusually happy temperament, and a most excellent heart. He has surrounded himself with a number of nieces (he says he cannot conceive of what use boys are in the world) whom he makes happy, and who make him so by their affection. They say he has the peculiar faculty of liking everything which he possesses, and everything that seeks his protection. He is an optimist, but not a conceited one.

Washington Irving invited me and my friends to his house for the following day, and in the forenoon I paid him a visit. His house or villa, which stands on the banks of the Hudson, resembles a peaceful idyll, thick masses of ivy clothe one portion of the white walls and garland the eaves. Fat cows graze in the meadow right before the window. Within, the room seemed full of summer warmth, and peace, and gave the appearance of something living. One felt that a cordial spirit, full of the best sentiments of the soul, lived and worked there. Washington Irving, although possessed of the politeness of a man of the world, and with abundant natural good temper, has nevertheless some of the natural shyness which so easily attaches itself to the author of the better and more refined type. A portrait which hangs in Washington Irving's drawing-room, and which was painted many years ago, represents him as a remarkably handsome man with dark eyes and hair—a head which might belong to a Spaniard. He must have been exceptionally handsome as a young man. He was engaged to a young lady of rare beauty and excellence;

it would have been difficult to meet with a handsomer pair. But she died, and Washington Irving never again sought another bride.

Ralph Waldo Emerson

I have just returned from a little journey to Concord, the oldest town in Massachusetts and the residence of Ralph Waldo Emerson.

Emerson, walking down the little avenue of spruce firs which leads from his house, came bare-headed in the storm to meet us. He is a quiet, nobly grave figure, his complexion pale, with strongly marked features and dark hair. He seemed to me a younger man, but not so handsome as I had imagined him: his exterior less fascinating, but more significant. He is a very singular character, but too cold and hyper-critical to please me entirely; a strong, clear eye, always looking out for an ideal, which he never finds realized on earth; discovering wants, short-comings, imperfections; and too strong and healthy himself to understand other peoples' weaknesses and sufferings, for he even despises suffering as a weakness unworthy of higher natures. This singularity of character leads one to suppose that he has never been ill: sorrows, however, he has had, and has felt them deeply, as some of his most beautiful poems prove; nevertheless he has only allowed himself to be bowed for a short time by those griefs—the deaths of two brothers and of a beautiful little boy, his oldest son. He also lost his first wife after having been married scarcely a year.

Emerson is now married for the second time and has three children. Mrs. Emerson has beautiful eyes, full of feeling, but she appears delicate, and is in character very different from her husband. He interested me without warming me.

P.S. I must tell you that I am not sure that I have judged rightly of Emerson. There is a higher nature in this man, and I must see more of him and understand him better.

Boston, January [1850]. Now I must tell you about Concord, and the sphynx there, Waldo Emerson, for I went to Concord five days ago. During the four days that I remained in Emerson's house I had a real enjoyment in the study of this strong, noble, eagle-like nature. I enjoyed the contemplation of him, in his demeanor, his expression, his mode of talking, and his every-day life, as I enjoy contemplating the calm flow of a river bearing along, between flowery shores, large and small vessels, and as I love to see the eagle circling in the clouds, resting upon them and its pinions. Emerson allows nothing to tear him away from his calm elevation, be it great or small, prosperity or adversity. His words are severe, his judgments often sharp and merciless, but his person is alike noble and pleasing, and his voice beautiful. One may quarrel with Emerson's thoughts, with his judgment, but not with himself. That which struck me most, as distinguishing him from other human beings, is *nobility*. He is a born nobleman.

William Lloyd Garrison

Another forenoon I saw Garrison, one of the champions of the Abolitionist cause who, in consequence, at a time of excitement was dragged by a mob through the streets of Boston, I believe with a halter round his neck as a malefactor. One sees in his beautiful countenance and clear, eagle eye that resolute spirit which makes the martyr. Speaking with him, I told him candidly that I thought the extravagance in the proceedings of the Abolitionists, their want of moderation, and the violent tone of their attacks could not benefit but rather must damage their cause. He replied with good temper, "We must demand the *whole* loaf, if we could hope to get one-half of it."

John Greenleaf Whittier

I had almost forgotten to tell you of a visit I had this evening from the Quaker poet, Whittier, one of the purest and most gifted of the poetical minds of the Northern States. He has a pleasing exterior; his figure is slender and tall; he has a beautiful head with refined features, black eyes full of fire, dark complexion, a fine smile, and a lively but nervous manner. Both soul and spirit have overstrained the nervous chords and affected the body. He belongs to those natures who would advance with firmness and joy to martyrdom in a good cause, and yet who are never comfortable in society, and look occasionally as though they would like to run out of the door.

Bronson Alcott

I have also been present at one of the "Conversations" of Alcott, the Transcendentalist, and have even taken part in the discourse. There were present from forty to fifty people, all seated on benches. Alcott sits in a pulpit with his face towards the people, and begins the conversation by reading something aloud. On this occasion it was from the writings of Pythagoras. He is a handsome man, of gentle manners, but a dreamer, whose Pythagorean wisdom will hardly make people wiser nowadays. He himself has lived for many years on bread, fruits, vegetables, and water; and this is what he wishes all other people to do; and thus fed, they would become, according to his theory, beautiful, good and happy beings. Sin is to be driven out by diet; and the sacred flood of enthusiasm would constantly flow through the human being purified and beautified by diet. Both the proposition and the conversation were in the clouds. Alcott drank water, and we drank—fog.

1851

A SLAVE AUCTION
by Fredrika Bremer

FREDRIKA BREMER was intensely interested in social reform. She utilized her books as vehicles to promote her ideas for improving the lot of the poor and downtrodden. This idea of helping the poor through her writing was so important to her that she refused several offers of marriage, preferring to remain a spinster so that she could devote all her time and energies to her crusade. The plight of the slaves in the ante-bellum South naturally enlisted her sympathies and aroused her indignation.

New Orleans, Louisiana, Jan. 1, 1851

On the 31st of December I went with my kind and estimable physician to witness a slave auction, which took place not far from my abode. It was held at one of the small auction-rooms which are found in various parts of New Orleans. The principal scene of these slave-auctions is a splendid rotunda, the magnificent dome of which is worthy to resound with songs of freedom. We entered a large and somewhat cold and dirty hall on the basement story of a house, where a great number of people were assembled. About twenty gentleman-like men stood in a half circle around a dirty wooden platform, which for the moment was unoccupied. On each side, by the wall, stood a number of black men and women, silent and serious. The whole assembly was silent, and it seemed to me as if a heavy gray cloud rested upon it.

A tall, stout man, with a gay and good-tempered aspect ascended the auction platform. He took the auctioneer's hammer in his hand, and addressed the assembly as follows: "The slaves which I now have to sell, for what price I can get, are a few home-slaves, all the property of one master. This gentleman, having given bond for a friend who afterward became bankrupt, has been obliged to meet his responsibilities by parting with his faithful servants. These slaves are thus sold, not in consequence of any faults which they possess, or for any deficiencies. They are all faithful and excellent servants, and nothing but hard necessity would have compelled their master to part with them."

After this he beckoned to a woman among the blacks to come forward, and he gave her his hand to mount upon the platform, where she remained standing beside him. She was a tall, well-grown mulatto, with a handsome but sorrowful countenance and a remarkably modest, noble demeanor. She bore on her arm a young, sleeping child, upon which during the whole ceremonial, she kept her eyes immovably riveted, with her head cast down. She wore a gray dress made to the throat, and a pale yellow handkerchief, checked with brown, was tied around her head. The auctioneer now began to laud this woman's good qualities, her skill and her abilities to the assembly. He praised her character, her good disposition, order, fidelity; her uncommon qualifications for taking care of a house: her piety, her talents, and remarked that the child which she bore at her breast, and which was to be sold with her, also increased her value. After this he shouted with a loud voice, "Now, gentlemen, how much for this very superior woman, this remarkable, etc., etc., and her child?"

He pointed with his outstretched arm and forefinger from one to another of the gentlemen who stood around, and first one and then another replied to his appeal with a short nod, and all the while he continued in this style: "Do you offer me five hundred dollars? Gentlemen, I am offered five hundred dollars for this superior woman and her child. She, with her child, is worth double that money. Five hundred and fifty, six hundred dollars. It is downright robbery! She would never have been sold at that price if her master had not been so unfortunate," etc., etc.

The hammer fell heavily; the woman and her child were sold for seven hundred dollars to one of those dark, silent, figures before her. Who he was; whether he was good or bad; whether he would lead her into tolerable or intolerable slavery—of all this, the bought and sold woman and mother knew as little as I did, neither to what part of the world he would take her. And the father of her child—where was he?

Next, a very dark young negro girl stepped upon the platform. She wore a bright yellow handkerchief tied very daintily around her head, so that the two ends stood out like wings, one on each side. Her figure was remarkably trim and neat, and her eyes glanced around the assembly both boldly and inquiringly. The auctioneer exalted her merits likewise, and then exclaimed, "How much for this very likely young girl?" She was soon sold, and, if I recollect rightly, for three hundred and fifty dollars.

After her a young man took his place on the platform. He was a mulatto and had a remarkably good countenance, expressive of gentleness and refinement. He had been a servant in his former master's family, had been brought up by him, was greatly beloved by him, and deserved to be so—a most excellent young man! He sold for six hundred dollars.

After this came an elderly woman, who had also one of those good-natured, excellent countenances so common among the black population, and whose demeanor showed that she, too, had been in the service of a good master, and, having been accustomed to gentle treatment, had become gentle and happy. All these slaves, as well as the young girl, who looked pert rather than good, bore the impression of having been accustomed to an affectionate family life.

And now, what was to be their future? How bitterly, if they fell into the hands of the wicked, would they feel the difference between then and now—how horrible would be their lot! No sermon, no anti-slavery oration could speak so powerfully against the institution of slavery as this slave-auction itself! The master had been good, the servants good also, attached and faithful, and yet they were sold to whoever would buy them—sold like brute beasts!

1851

A MINING TOWN IN THE GOLD RUSH
by J. D. Bothwick

In 1851 the great American dream was to go to California, find gold, and get rich overnight. Adventurous men from every walk of life left their friends, their work and their families to try their luck in the gold fields.

J. D. Bothwick, a visiting Scot, caught the gold fever and traveled to California with the rest. Like many others he was unsuccessful, and after some months in a mining town he gave up prospecting and returned home.

The town of Placerville—or Hangtown (It received its name of Hangtown while yet in its infancy from the number of malefactors who had there expiated their crimes at the hands of Judge Lynch.), as it was commonly called—consisted of one long straggling street of clapboard houses and log cabins, built in a hollow at the side of a creek, and surrounded by high and steep hills.

The diggings had been exceedingly rich—men used to pick the chunks of gold out of the crevices of the rocks in the ravines with no other tool than a bowie-knife; but these days had passed, and now the whole surface of the surrounding country showed the amount of real hard work which had been done. The beds of the numerous ravines which wrinkle the faces of the hills, the bed of the creek, and all the little flats alongside of it, were a confused mass of heaps of dirt and piles of stones lying around the innumerable holes, about six feet deep, from which they had been thrown out. The original course of the creek was completely obliterated, its waters being distributed into numberless little ditches, and from them conducted into the "long toms" of the miners through canvas hoses, looking like immensely long slimy sea-serpents.

Along the whole length of the creek, as far as one could see, on the banks of the ravines, in the middle of the principal and only street of the town, and even inside some of the houses, were parties of miners, numbering from three or four to a dozen, all hard at work, some laying into it with picks, some shovelling the dirt into the "long toms," or with long-handled shovels washing the dirt thrown in, and throwing out the stones, while others were working pumps or baling water out of the holes with buckets. There was a continual noise and clatter, as mud, dirt, stones, and water, were thrown about in all directions; and the men, dressed in ragged clothes and big boots, wielding picks and shovels, and rolling big rocks about, were all working as if for their lives, going into it with a will, and a degree of energy, not usually seen among laboring men. It was altogether a scene which conveyed the idea of hard work in the fullest sense of the words, and in comparison with which a gang of Railway navvies would have seemed to be merely a party of gentlemen amateurs playing at working *pour passer le temps*.

A stroll through the village revealed the extent to which the ordinary comforts of life were attainable. The gambling houses, of which there were three or four, were of course the largest and most conspicuous buildings, their mirrors, chandeliers, and other decorations, suggesting a style of life totally at variance with the outward indications of everything around them.

The street itself was in many places knee-deep in mud, and was plentifully strewed with old boots, hats, and shirts, old sardine boxes, worn out pots and kettles, old ham-bones, broken picks and shovels, and other rubbish too various to particularise. Here and there, in the middle of the street, was a square hole about six feet deep in which one miner was digging, while another was baling the water out with a bucket, and a third, sitting alongside the heap of dirt which had been dug up, was washing it in a rocker. Wagons, drawn by six or eight mules or oxen, were navigating along the street, or discharging their strangely-assorted cargoes at the various stores; and men in picturesque rags, with large muddy boots, long beards and brown faces, were the only inhabitants to be seen.

I met a San Francisco friend in Hangtown practising his profession as a doctor, who very hospitably offered me quarters in his cabin, which I gladly accepted. The accommodation was not very luxurious, being merely six feet of the floor on which to spread my blankets. Three or four miners were also inmates of the doctor's cabin. They were going to work a claim about two miles up the creek from Hangtown. As they wanted another hand to work their "long tom" with them, I very readily joined their party. For several days we worked the place but the claim did not prove rich enough to satisfy us, so we abandoned it, and went "prospecting," which means looking about for a more likely place.

A "prospector" goes out with a pick and shovel and a wash-pan; and to test the richness of a place he digs down till he reaches the dirt in which it may be expected that the gold will be found; and washing out a panful of this, he can easily calculate, from the amount of gold he finds in it, how much could be taken out in a day's work.

To establish one's claim to a piece of ground, all that was requisite was to leave upon it a pick or shovel, or other mining tool. The extent of ground allowed to each individual varied in different diggings from ten to thirty feet square.

1858

A MEETING WITH LINCOLN
by Carl Schurz

CARL SCHURZ was a young German liberal who came to the United States with his wife in 1852 because the American Constitution with its ideal of liberty and democracy was close to his own thought.

By 1858 he was playing a leading role in the young Republican party and was taking an active part in the Illinois campaign where Abraham Lincoln and Stephen A. Douglas were staging their famous debates.

Later Schurz became a successful and influential journalist, as well as the author of some outstanding books, among them *The Reminiscences of Carl Schurz,* from which the following excerpt is taken.

On the evening before the day of the debate, I was on a railroad car bound for Quincy. The car in which I traveled was full of men who discussed the absorbing question with great animation.

All at once after the train had left a way station, I observed a great commotion among my fellow-passengers, many of whom jumped from their seats and pressed eagerly around a tall man who had just entered the car. They addressed him in the most familiar style: "Hello, Abe! How are you?" and so on. And he responded in the same manner: "Good evening, Ben! How are you, Joe?" "Why," exclaimed my companion, a committee-man, "there's Lincoln himself!" He pressed through the crowd and introduced me to Abraham Lincoln, whom I then saw for the first time.

I must confess that I was somewhat startled by his appearance. There he stood, overtopping by several inches all those surrounding him. Although measuring something over six feet myself, I had, standing quite near to him, to throw my head backwards in order to look into his eyes. That swarthy face with its strong features, its deep furrows, and its benignant, melancholy eyes, is now familiar to every American by numberless pictures. At that time it was clean-shaven, and looked even more haggard and careworn than later when it was framed in whiskers.

On his head he wore a somewhat battered "stove-pipe" hat. His neck emerged, long and sinewy, from a white collar turned down over a thin black necktie. His lank, ungainly body was clad in a rusty black dress coat with sleeves that should have been longer; but his arms appeared so long that the sleeves of a "store" coat could hardly be expected to cover them all the way down to the wrists. His black trousers, too, permitted a very full view of his large feet. On his left arm he carried a grey woolen shawl, which evidently served him for an overcoat in chilly weather. His left hand held a cotton umbrella of the bulging kind, and also a black satchel that bore the marks of long and hard usage. His right he had kept free for handshaking, of which there was no end until everybody in the car seemed to be satisfied.

He received me with an off-hand cordiality, like an old acquaintance, having been informed of what I was doing in the campaign, and we sat down together. In a somewhat high-pitched but pleasant voice he began to talk to me, telling me much about the points he and Douglas had made in the debates at different places, and about those he intended to make at Quincy on the morrow.

When, in a tone of perfect ingenuousness, he asked me—a young beginner in politics—what I thought about this and that, I should have felt myself very much honored by his confidence, had he permitted me to regard him as a great man. But he talked in so simple and familiar a strain, and his manner and homely phrase were so absolutely free from any semblance of self-consciousness or pretension to superiority, that I soon felt as if I had known him all my life and we had long been close friends. He interspersed our conversation with all sorts of quaint stories, each of which had a witty point applicable to the subject in hand, and not seldom concluding an argument in such a manner that nothing more was to be said. He seemed to enjoy his own jests in a child-like way, for his unusually sad-looking eyes would kindle in a merry twinkle, and he, himself, led in the laughter; and his laugh was so genuine, hearty, and contagious that nobody could fail to join in it.

When we arrived at Quincy, we found a large number of friends waiting for him, and there was much hand-shaking. Then they got him into a carriage, much against his wish, for he said that he would prefer to "foot it to Browning's," an old friend's house, where he was to have supper and a quiet night.

The great debate took place in the afternoon on the open square where a large, pine-board platform had been built for the committee of arrangements, the speakers, and the persons they wished to have with them. As the champions arrived they were demonstratively cheered by their adherents. The presiding officer called the meeting to order and announced the program of proceedings. Mr. Lincoln was to open with an allowance of one hour, and Senator Douglas was to follow with a speech of one hour and a half, and Mr. Lincoln was to speak half an hour in conclusion. Mr. Lincoln had none of those physical advantages which usually are thought to be very desirable, if not necessary, to the orator. His voice was not musical, rather high-keyed, and apt to turn into a shrill treble in moments of excitement; but it was not positively disagreeable. It had an exceedingly penetrating, far-reaching quality. The looks of the audience convinced me that every word he spoke was understood at the remotest edges of the vast assembly. His gesture was awkward. He swung his long arms sometimes in a very ungraceful manner. Now and then he would, to give particular emphasis to a point, bend his knees and body with a sudden downward jerk, and then shoot up again with a vehemence that raised him to his tip-toes and made him look much taller than he really was—a manner of enlivening a speech which at that time was, and perhaps still is, not unusual in the West, but which he succeeded in avoiding at a later period.

There was, however, in all he said, a tone of earnest truthfulness, of elevated, noble sentiment, and of kindly sympathy, which added greatly to the strength of his argument, and became, as in the course of his speech he touched upon the moral side of the question in debate, powerfully impressive. Even when attacking his opponent with keen satire or invective, which, coming from any other speaker, would have sounded bitter and cruel, there was still a certain something in his utterance making his hearers feel that those thrusts came from a reluctant heart, and that he would much rather have treated his foe as a friend.

THE CIVIL WAR
AND THE RECONSTRUCTION ERA

1862

THE FEDERAL SOLDIER
by Anthony Trollope

ANTHONY TROLLOPE was the novelist son of the Frances Trollope whose reminiscences of America, *Domestic Manners of the Americans,* had caused so much hard feeling on this side of the Atlantic. Anthony, who had remained in school in England during his mother's Cincinnati adventure, was already a well-known author when he made his own trip to the United States thirty-four years later as a correspondent for a British newspaper. A big, bluff, John Bull type of Englishman, Trollope proved to be an honest and fair-minded reporter, more reliable, if less entertaining, than his spirited mother.

There were only a thousand soldiers at Cairo [Illinois] when we were there;—that is a thousand stationed in the Cairo sheds. Two regiments passed through the place during the time, getting out of one steamer on to another, or passing from the railway into boats. One of these regiments passed before me down the slope of the river-bank, and the men as a body seemed to be healthy. Very many were drunk, and all were mud-clogged up to their shoulders and very caps. It must

111

be understood that these soldiers, the volunteers, had never been made subject to any discipline as to cleanliness. They wore their hair long. Their hats or caps, though all made in some military form and with some military appendance, were various and ill-assorted. They all were covered with loose, thick, blue-gray great-coats, which no doubt were warm and wholesome, but which from their looseness and colour seemed to be peculiarly susceptible of receiving and showing a very large amount of mud. Their boots were always good; but each man was shod as he liked. Many wore heavy over-boots coming up at the leg; boots in which a man would be not at all unfortunate to find himself hunting; but from these, or from their highlows, shoes, or whatever they might wear, the mud had never been even scraped. These men were all warmly clothed, but clothed apparently with an endeavor to contract as much mud as might be possible.

Want of discipline and dirt have, no doubt, been the great faults of the regiments generally, and the latter drawback may probably be included in the former. These men have not been accustomed to act under the orders of superiors, and when they entered on the service hardly recognized the fact that they would have to do so in ought else than in their actual drill and fighting. It is impossible to conceive any class of men to whom the necessary discipline of a soldier would come with more difficulty than to an American citizen. The whole training of his life has been against it. He has never known respect for a master, or reverence for men of a higher rank than himself. He has probably been made to work hard for his wages, —harder than an Englishman works,—but he has been his employer's equal. The language between them has been the language of equals, and their arrangement as to labour and wages has been a contract between equals. If he did not work he would not get his money,—and perhaps not if he did. Under these circumstances he has made his fight with the world; but those circumstances have never taught him that special deference to a superior, which is the first essential of a soldier's duty. But probably in no respect would that difficulty be so severely felt as in all matters appertaining to personal habits. Here at any rate the man would expect to be still his own master, acting for himself and independent of all outer control. Our English Hodge, when taken from the plough to the camp, would, probably, submit without a murmur to soap and water and a barber's shear; he would have received none of that education which would prompt him to rebel against such ordinances; but the American citizen, who for a while expects to shake hands with the captain whenever he sees him, and is astonished when he learns that he must not offer him drinks, cannot at once be brought to understand that he is to be treated like a child in the nursery;—that he must change his shirt so often, wash himself at such and such intervals, and go through a certain process of cleansing his outward garments daily. It is very bad that soldiers should be dirty, bad also that they should treat their captains with familiarity and desire to exchange drinks with the majors. But even discipline is not everything; and discipline will come at last even to the American soldiers, when the necessity for it is made apparent. But these volunteers have great military virtues. They are intelligent, zealous in their cause, handy with arms, willing enough to work at all military duties, and personally brave.

GLIMPSES OF SLAVERY
by Edward Dicey

EDWARD DICEY was a distinguished journalist, editor of the London *News* and the London *Observer*. In 1862 he came to the United States as correspondent for the *Spectator*.

An expert and observant reporter, he sent reports back to England that were fair to the North as well as to the more popular South and that correctly estimated the strength and future importance of America.

Of course we all know, or if we do not know it is not for want of telling, that the slaves are contented and happy, and have no wish for freedom. It may be so; but if so, it is hard to explain why the papers of the Slave States are filled with advertisements of runaway slaves. Every day, for instance, in the *Baltimore Sun,* which I used to see constantly at Washington, there appeared a row of advertisements, of which the following may be taken as types:—

3d March, 1862

25 dollars reward. Ran away, March 2d, from the farm of Mrs. S. B. Mayo, in Anne Arundel county, negro boy, John Stewart. He is 19 or 20 years of age; 5 feet 9 or 10 inches high; very prominent mouth and large front teeth; light *complexion; has a stupid look when spoken too; his father lives in Annapolis. Any one who will arrest and secure him in jail can receive the above reward.*

T. H. Gaither, Howard Co.

13th March, 1862

200 dollars reward. Ran away from the subscriber, living in the upper part of Calvert county, in September last, my negro man Thomas, who calls himself Thomas Jones. He is about 5 feet 6 to

9 inches high; dark chestnut colour; stout and well built; large white teeth; with full suit of hair (plaited when he left home); the whites of his eyes show very much when spoken to; had on white cloth peajacket, dark cloth pantaloons and cloth cap. I have no doubt that he is in or about Washington or Bladensburgh, as he left a day or two before Colonel Cowdin's regiment left; or, if in Baltimore, he is with the Jones' or Kayes', his free relatives. I will give the above reward, if taken out of the State of Maryland or the district of Columbia, or any county of the State except Calvert; and fifty dollars if taken in Calvert county. In either case, to be delivered to me or secured in jail, so that I get him again.

Jonathan Y. Barber

But to me the saddest of all these exhibitions of human depravity was contained in an advertisement which appeared for days together:—

15th March, 1862
Ran away from subscriber, 13th March, negro woman, Ellen, aged about forty years, and her boy Joe, aged seven years. They are both yellow colour. Ellen has a defect in one eye; Joe is bright yellow. I will pay a liberal award for their arrest.

Joshua M. Bosley

At last the advertisements stopped. Was the search given up as useless? or, was the liberal reward earned and paid. God knows.

1863

A MEETING WITH ROBERT E. LEE

From the Diary of Lieutenant Colonel James Fremantle

LIEUTENANT COLONEL JAMES FREMANTLE of the famous Coldstream Guards decided to take a "busman's holiday" by spending his leave in America and having a professional look at the most interesting military engagement of his day: the American Civil War.

Like most Englishmen, Fremantle sympathized with the underdog and he therefore chose to see the war from the Confederate side. He marched into battle with the Southern armies and was at Gettysburg when Lee, magnificent in defeat as in victory, was attempting to rally his discouraged troops.

When the battle was over, Fremantle, whose leave had expired, made his way through the Union lines to New York, where he caught a ship back to England.

30th June, 1863

General Lee is, almost without exception, the handsomest man of his age I ever saw. He is fifty-six years old, tall, broad-shouldered, very well made, well set up—a thorough soldier in appearance; and his manners are most courteous and full of dignity. He is a perfect gentleman in every respect. I imagine no man has so few enemies, or is so universally esteemed. He has none of the small vices, such as smoking, drinking, chewing, or swearing, and his bitterest enemy never accused him of any of the greater ones.

He generally wears a well-worn long gray jacket, a high black felt hat, and blue trousers tucked into his Wellington boots. I never saw him carry arms; and the only mark of his military rank are the three stars on his collar. He rides a handsome horse, which is extremely well groomed. He himself is very neat in his dress and person, and in the most arduous marches he always looks smart and clean.

In the old army he was always considered one of its best officers; and at the outbreak of these troubles, he was lieutenant colonel of the 2d cavalry. He was a rich man, but his fine estate was one of the first to fall into the enemy's hands. I believe he has never slept in a house since he had commanded the Virginian army, and he invariably declines all offers of hospitality, for fear the person offering it may afterwards get into trouble for having sheltered the Rebel General.

With Lee at Gettysburg

If Longstreet's conduct [at Gettysburg] was admirable, that of General Lee was perfectly sublime. He was engaged in rallying and in encouraging the broken troops, and was riding about a little in front of the wood, quite alone—the whole of his staff being engaged in a similar manner further to the rear. His face, which is always placid and cheerful, did not show signs of the slightest disappointment, care, or annoyance; and he was addressing to every soldier he met a few words of encouragement, such as, "All this will come right in the end; we'll talk it over afterwards; but in the meantime, all good men must rally. We want all good and true men just now," etc.

He spoke to all the wounded men that passed him, and the slightly wounded he exhorted "to bind up hurts and take up a musket" in this emergency. Very few failed to answer his appeal, and I saw many badly wounded men take off their hats and cheer him. He said to me, "This has been a sad day for us, Colonel—a sad day; but we can't expect always to gain victories." He was also kind enough to advise me to get into some more sheltered position, as the shells were bursting around us with considerable frequency.

Notwithstanding the misfortune which had so suddenly befallen him, General Lee seemed to observe everything, however trivial. When a mounted officer began licking his horse for shying at the bursting of a shell, he called out, "Don't whip him, Captain; don't whip him. I've got just such another foolish horse myself, and whipping does no good."

I happened to see a man lying flat on his face in a small ditch, and I remarked that I didn't think he seemed dead; this drew General Lee's attention to the man, who commenced groaning dismally. Finding appeals to his patriotism of no avail, General Lee had him ignominiously set on his legs by some neighboring gunners.

I saw General Willcox (an officer who wears a short round jacket and a battered straw hat) come up to him, and explain almost crying, the state of his brigade. General Lee immediately shook hands with him and said cheerfully, *"Never mind, General, all this has been* MY *fault—*it is I that have lost this fight, and you must help me out of it in the best way you can."

In this manner I saw General Lee encourage and reanimate his somewhat dispirited troops, and magnanimously take upon his own shoulders the whole weight of the repulse. It was impossible to look at him or to listen to him without feeling the strongest admiration, and I never saw any man fail him except the man in the ditch.

1863

BLOCKADE RUNNERS
by Fitzgerald Ross

AT THE OUTBREAK of the Civil War, Lincoln proclaimed a blockade of the Southern coast with the dual objective of stopping the South from exporting its cotton to Europe and preventing it from importing the munitions, medical supplies and clothing it so desperately needed. Although it was unsuccessful during the early days of the war, the blockade had become highly effective by 1863. The picture painted by Fitzgerald Ross, an Englishman who had served as a Captain of Hussars in the Imperial Austrian Service and also had come on a busman's holiday to take a look at the Civil War, must be somewhat discounted because of the pro-Southern sympathies of the author.

Wilmington is at present the most important port of entry in the South, and the custom-house receipts, both here and at Charleston, last year, far exceeded anything they had ever been during a similar period before the war. There were about a dozen blockade-running steamers lying at the wharves, loading cotton, and unloading all manner of stores brought from Bermuda and Nassau. Besides cotton, the chief exports are tobacco and rosin.

A day or two after our arrival, we went down to Fort Fisher, at the mouth of the Cape Fear River, the Commandant, Colonel Lamb, taking us down in his boat. Going down, we met three steamers coming up the river, having successfully run the blockade, the Hansa, the Lucy, and the Bendigo. We exchanged cheers as they passed us; but the great sight is when they come up to the wharves. They all dress up with flags as if for a victory; and as the ships which belong to the same company do the same, the spectacle is very gay. The cheering, too, is vociferous, and all those who have any interest in the vessel must, no doubt, feel extremely comfortable, as every successful trip brings an enormous profit. The moon is the blockade-runner's greatest enemy; but these vessels to-day had come in, notwithstanding the moon, which did not set till three o'clock in the morning. Fort Fisher consists of a long line of forts and batteries of all sorts and sizes. A fleet trying to get into the river would have to run the gauntlet of these batteries for more than a mile, and would most assuredly suffer very severely in the attempt.

In the far distance we could see two Federal men-of-war keeping up a nominal blockade. They always remain at a respectful distance, for if they come within three or four miles, Colonel Lamb is apt to make targets of them and his gun practice is very accurate. They seldom catch a blockade-runner going in or out, but if on the high seas they can capture a ship laden with a suspicious cargo, they condemn her as a prize without more ado; and as the vessels all sail under the supposed protection of the British flag, the owners never have any redress.

Sometimes a vessel gets "beached," as on a dark night it is very difficult exactly to hit the point for which they are steering. This accident happened to the Ceres, a noble double screw steamer, that was making her first voyage. The Yankees coming up in the morning, the ship had to be set on fire; her mail and a small portion of passengers' luggage were saved, but the cargo was lost. Some of the passengers had had a narrow escape, the ebbing tide having carried their boat far out to sea, but eventually all got safe to land.

1865

THE END OF THE WAR
by Régis de Trobriand

Régis de Trobriand was born in France but emigrated as a young man to America, where he became a naturalized citizen. At the outbreak of the Civil War, he was elected Colonel of the 55th New York Militia, more generally known as the Guard Lafayette because most of its members were of French descent.

"The condition made me, as a candidate [for Colonel], was that I should lead the regiment to the front," General de Trobriand writes. "The condition I made on accepting the command was that the regiment should follow me to the front."

Both conditions were met and the regiment fought gallantly throughout the war. By the time peace came, its commanding officer, Régis de Trobriand, had been made a Brevet Major-General.

In France, the American Civil War had been both misrepresented and misunderstood. In order to rectify this situation General de Trobriand decided to write an account of the war as he himself had seen it. "I have limited myself to those things which I have seen myself," he writes in the preface to his book, "I relate them not as a Frenchman who has taken part in a foreign war, but as an American who has fought for the country of his adoption and for the institutions of his choice."

Observant, clear-sighted and endowed with a sense of humor, General de Trobriand gives a vivid and unforgettable picture of the American Civil War and the officers and men who fought in the Army of the Potomac.

The battle of the 6th April [1865] known generally under the name of the battle of Sailor's Creek, gave the *coup de grace* to Lee's army. Worn out by fatigue and hunger, exposed to every privation and every discouragement, these twenty-six to twenty-eight thousand men were no longer in condition to defend themselves. A portion was without arms; the remainder was only capable henceforth of those spasmodic efforts in which a mortal agony is extinguished.

During the night of the 6th and 7th the enemy continued his movements. At daylight, Humphreys was already in pursuit. In the rapidity of the march, I passed by a crossroad I should have taken, and soon, having some suspicions on the subject, I halted, while my aid sought for information. A general, followed by some staff officers and an escort of cavalry, came up the road near which I halted. Those around me said, "It is Sheridan!" which excited my curiosity.

General Sheridan is of medium height, stout and vigorous; with a soldierly air. He, at that time, wore his hair brushed up and his moustache *au naturel;* his eyes are black and bright; his look denotes great quickness of perception and temperament. His features are regular; his open countenance denotes a frank decision of character.

He halted near me, saluting me, calling me by my name as if we had been old acquaintances, and as soon as I had made known to him my doubt as to which road I ought to take, in a few words he put before me very clearly my line of march. I left him immediately, in order to repair the delay of some minutes, and at the hour announced we reached High Bridge.

That is a magnificent viaduct of twenty-one arches, crossing the valley of the Appomattox from one hill to the other. When we presented ourselves at one end, the enemy, who had just crossed over, was setting fire to the other. We had to throw a pontoon bridge across the river. A strong detachment, armed with axes hurried to the fire. The upper bridge, on which was the railroad, was saved by the sacrifice of a third span, and the lower bridge was open for our trains, after some slight repairs.

The Second Division crossed over first. General Barlow was in command. The enemy's rearguard was still on the hills. Barlow had scarcely reached the further bank when he was sent to Framville. General Humphreys, with my division and that of Miles, continued energetically to pursue the greater part of the Confederates by the road to Appomattox Court House. We came up with them five or six miles further on. The day was passing away. A charge was ordered of three regiments of the First Division. It was repulsed with loss. We had to do with too strong a force.

We were thus compelled to put off the renewal of the attack till the next day. But the enemy did not wait. He commenced his march during the night, and the grand chase began again, with eagerness, at daylight.

We advanced in three columns, picking up all that was left behind of the Confederate army. This remnant was breaking up more and more, leaving its stragglers in the woods, in the fields, and along the roadside. Animals and men were yielding to exhaustion. The wagons were left in the ruts; the cannon abandoned in the thickets or buried in holes, hurriedly dug. The places were marked for those who should be charged with the duty of bringing off the pieces, and, without halting, we pushed forward, "on a hot trail," like hounds who are coming upon their quarry.

April 9, 1865.—Forward again early in the morning, always on the heels of the enemy's rearguard. A vigorous cannonade and a musketry fire are heard from three or four miles in advance. Instinctively everybody cries: "There is Sheridan! Bully for Sheridan!"

This was the last convulsive effort of the rebel army in the throes of death. The circle of steel had closed about it, and the army of Lee had nothing else to do but either to surrender or perish drowned in its own blood. It surrendered. The white flag was flown along its lines, and General Grant received the following note from General Lee:

"General,—I received your note of this morning on the picket line, whither I had come to meet you, and ascertain definitely what terms were embraced in your proposal of yesterday with reference to the surrender of this army. I now ask an interview in accordance with the offer contained in your offer of yesterday for that purpose."

The interview was granted, and the two generals met in a house at Appomattox Court House.

Immediately an order from General Meade announced to us that, on account of the situation of affairs, hostilities were suspended for one hour. Half an hour later we were advised that the truce was prolonged till two o'clock in the afternoon.

At exactly two, our division moved out. But my first brigade had not made a quarter of a mile when I again received orders to halt.

Soon a carriage is signalled drawn by four horses, with a white flag floating over it. Everybody hurried to the borders of the road. What can it be? Civilians in frock coats and with chimney-pot hats! It is soon made known that it is a Judge Ould and a Colonel Heath, commissioners for the exchange of prisoners for the Confederates. Since entrance to our lines is permitted them, everything is doubtless settled. Cheers began to break out along the line. These gentlemen salute and pass on.

The carriage having gone on its road, impatience rises to fever heat. Nothing settled yet? There must be some trick intended. If they do not wish to surrender, all right! Let us go in at once.

All at once a tempest of hurrahs shook the air along the front of our line. General Meade is coming at a gallop from Appomattox Court House. He has raised his cap and uttered a few words: LEE HAS SURRENDERED! Mad hurrahs fill the air like the rolling of thunder, in the fields, in the woods, along the roads, and are prolonged in echo amongst the trains, which in the distance are following the Sixth Corps.

General Meade leaves the road and passes through my division. The men swarm out to meet him, surrounding his horse. Hurrah for General Meade! Again, Hurrah! and on all sides, Hurrah! The enthusiasm gains the officers of his staff, who cry out like all the rest, waving their hats. Caps fly into the air; the colors are waved and saluted, shaking their glorious rags in the breeze; all the musicians fill the air with the joyous notes of "Yankee Doodle" and the sonorous strains of "Hail Columbia."

All the hopes of four years at last realized; all the fears dissipated, all perils disappeared; all the privations, all the sufferings, all the misery ended; the intoxication of triumph; the joy at the near return to the domestic hearth,—for all this, one single burst of enthusiasm did not suffice. So the hurrahs and the cries of joy were prolonged until night.

1867

THE SOUTH AFTER THE WAR
by F. Barham Zincke

F. BARHAM ZINCKE, Vicar of Wherstead and Chaplain in Ordinary to Queen Victoria, made a tour of the United States during the winter of 1867. It is interesting to read his impressions of the South after the war and to note that two of the states which seemed to him to have suffered the most are today states where the adjustment to integration is having great difficulties.

I have been frequently asked what I found was the condition of the South.

The fact that first forces itself on the eye in the towns, and often in the rural districts you pass through, is that there are multitudes of negroes looking about, doing nothing. You see them at every station. When you come to make inquiries as to what they are doing, and how they subsist, and generally as to the state of the country, you are told that they are to be found in shoals in every town where there is a Freedman's bureau. They expect something from the Bureau; and, like so many coloured Micawbers, are drawn to the towns in the hope that something will turn up. So in the towns; but that in the country districts, where there is no power to restrain the idle and ill-disposed, things are in an actively bad condition—that this class has taken to stealing, and has not left on many properties a sweet potato or head of maize, or the pig that would have fed upon them—that they have made a clean sweep of everything edible. As to the state of the whites, that their condition is far more dreadful both to bear and to contemplate, for the blacks, as soon as they please to do the work they are accustomed to, may escape from their present distress, but, that the tens of thousands of white families, who lately were living in affluence and refinement, not knowing what it was to want anything or to do anything for themselves, are now in a state of abject penury, positively of starvation; that many are without the means of procuring hominy and salt pork, the humblest fare in the country. And about this point there can be no doubt; for you have as evidence of the statement not only what Southerners say, but, as I afterwards found on returning to New York, the corroborative evidence of those good Northern people who are themselves subscribing largely to keep these destitute Southern families alive.

But the first observation to be made in these statements is, that they cannot be equally applicable to all the very differently circumstanced States of the late Southern Confederacy.

For instance, the State of Missouri, which is one of the most fertile in the country, and by its climate thoroughly adapted to the Northern farm-system, was instantly benefited by the abolition of slavery. Tennessee and Kentucky will soon be in the same position, for both may very well be cultivated by white labour. Texas was even at the moment very slightly affected by the change; and will now become a more attractive field than ever for white immigration. Here cattle-breeding is the chief occupation, which is one that does not at all require slave labour. Virginia, having passed through all the distress which is implied by the passage from the estate to the farm system, will emerge from its present distress a far richer and more populous State than it was before. General Lee's son, and many others of the noble Virginia race, have already set the example, and are themselves holding the plough and doing all the work of the farm with their own hands.

In Georgia, particularly in the upper part of the State, where the ground rises considerably, I heard and saw that successful efforts were being made to effect the change from the estate to the farm system; and, instead of trusting entirely to cotton, to try what could be done by growing wheat and maize, the latter to be turned into pork—in short to do whatever could be done to adapt their industry to existing circumstances. Florida at present is rather occupied by wild deer than by man. Mrs. Harriet Beecher Stowe, however, the writer of "Uncle Tom's Cabin," has gone to Florida with her brother, Mr. Charles Beecher, for the purpose of attempting the cultivation of the sugar cane with free labour.

North Carolina is endeavoring to follow the example of its neighbours, Virginia and Georgia. Arkansas, which was settled chiefly by the sons of Georgia planters, is showing much of the Georgian spirit. In Alabama great efforts had been made to re-establish the cultivation of cotton on the basis of freedom; and things were promising well, when at the end of 1867 the price of cotton, by a concurrence of adverse accidents fell to 15 cents at Liverpool. This depression to a point below the cost of production in any part of the world, was felt by most of those who attend to these matters, to be only a temporary mishap.

There now remain unmentioned only the three States of South Carolina, Louisiana and Mississippi. As far as I could judge, South Carolina was bitterly and hopelessly crushed. Its best estates were in the Sea Islands, which, as they were very fertile and their produce fetched exceptionally high prices, were densely inhabited with blacks; in many of them, however, no white man could live with impunity. Under these circumstances it might have been expected that as soon as the negroes were emancipated, they would take possession of the land in these islands. And so it happened in most of the unhealthy ones; while in those that were healthy, the original proprietors equally lost their property by confiscation or forfeiture. The result of this, and of the other losses that arose out of the war, is that throughout South Carolina the most abject and irrecoverable poverty reigns precisely where formerly there was most abundant wealth.

In Louisiana, also, things were so bad that it was hardly possible to see how they could be worse. In New Orleans I found families who formerly had lived in noble mansions and exercised a grand hospitality, now occupying quiet lodgings. In some instances I knew of several families clubbing together, and living as it were in common. But here there was a great difference—hope was not dead; they talked confidently of reestablishment, at all events, of their sugar industry, and of the trade of the city. I saw several sugar estates not far from New Orleans, the very costly machinery upon which had been destroyed during the war.

As far as I could see and hear, the State of Mississippi also was in a very bad way. This seemed to arise from two causes. A larger proportion of the white inhabitants than is the case elsewhere belong to the class called in the South "mean whites." And then the planters are unable to borrow what is requisite for enabling them to work their plantations. No one will lend them a cent. This is but a natural consequence of the act of repudiation they adopted at the instigation of Mr. J. Davis, late President of the Southern Confederacy, and whom this State has either the honour or the dishonour of reckoning among her best known men.

If we form our estimate of the conditions of the South from considering the condition of its means of communication, we shall find it bad indeed. While I was there, some of its main lines of railway were running only one passenger train a day. What ruin and desolation may be read in this single fact, when one remembers that a few years back the value of the raw produce exported from the Southern States amounted to between fifty and sixty million pounds a year!

One of the most lamentable results of the great cataclysm that ensued in the close of the war, has been that almost a complete end has been put to the education of Southern children. Formerly many were sent to the North, but now parents have neither the inclination nor the means to continue this practice. In the South itself schools did not abound; and of those which existed before the war the greater number have followed the fate of so many other Southern things. Some effort is being made to remedy this.

Formerly it would have been thought impossible to harmonise such discordant elements as the North and the South. Could they ever be fused into a single homogeneous people? Down to the times of our fathers, it would have been quite impossible. Each would have kept only to his own region, and known no influence but those which were native to it. But now we have changed all that. A few threads of wire overhead, and a few bars of iron on the levelled ground, will do all that is wanted. For extreme remoteness, they have substituted so close a contiguity that the North and South can now talk together. Men are what their ideas are. And every morning these two peoples have the same ideas and the same facts, put in the same words before them. The wire-threads overhead do this. And if a Southern man thinks that his interests call him to the North, or a Northern man that his call him to the South, the railway will transport them hither and thither in a moment. Everyone can foresee the result—that there must, sooner or later, be one homogeneous people.

A RECONSTRUCTED NATION

1875

THE FREE LUNCH
by Jacques Offenbach

JACQUES OFFENBACH (1819–1880) was a celebrated composer of operettas and one opera, *The Tales of Hoffmann,* whose music is still popular today. Born in Cologne, Germany, the young Offenbach was sent to Paris when he was fourteen years old to study the violoncello. He loved France so much that he stayed there for the rest of his life, first as a member of the orchestra of the Opéra Comique, then as Conductor of the Théâtre Français.

In 1875, at the height of his fame, Jacques Offenbach came to America as guest conductor with various American orchestras. Talented, gay and irrepressibly witty, he had a highly successful tour and, on his return to France, wrote a highly successful and delightful book on his American experiences, *Offenbach in America.*

Several New York restaurants serve meals for nothing—provided you take a drink, even if it only costs ten cents. On Sundays, when, thanks to the police, the restaurants dare not serve drinks, it is all the better for the consumer. Lunch is served as usual, and I can state this as a fact, having seen it at the Brunswick myself; and they say that living is expensive in America.

And it must not be supposed that this gratuitous meal is composed of mere trifles. Here is a bill of fare, copied on the spot:

Ham
An enormous piece of roast-beef
Pork and beans
Potato salad
Olives, pickles, etc.
Cheese
Crackers

Wholesome and abundant fare as may be seen. The most substantial part is the roast-beef, from which the guests are privileged to cut, themselves, such slices as they like.

A large pile of plates stands on a side-board, convenient free lunch, together with forks and knives in abundance; but the guests, as a rule, prefer using their own fingers; some going so far as to help themselves by the handful out of the salad-bowl. I shudder still, just to think of it!

The head-waiter, to whom I expressed my horror and astonishment, tried his best to soothe my feelings.

"This offends us less than it does you. *Time is money,* you see; and these gentlemen are in such a hurry!"

Gilmore's Garden was a popular concert hall in New York City that had been "newly and wonderfully" redecorated in honor of Offenbach's visit.

I breakfast hurriedly, for my one wish, my one desire since arriving, is to see the famous covered Garden where I am about to display my talents; I hastened then to Gilmore's Garden.

Imagine a vast covered garden. In the centre of a great mass of tropical plants stands the stage, large enough to accommodate an orchestra of a hundred to a hundred and twenty musicians. All around are grass-plots, shrubbery and flower beds, among which the public circulate. Facing the entry is a large cascade, which imitates Niagara Falls during the interludes. The corners of the Garden are occupied by little Swiss cottages, which can hold seven or eight persons and which advantageously supply the place of boxes in a theatre. A large gallery, with ordinary boxes and tiers of seats, afford facilities for those who like seeing and hearing from an elevation, to satisfy their taste.

The hall has a capacity of eight to nine thousand persons. It is brilliantly lit up; colored glasses are hung in festoons of the most picturesque effect.

1876

SUMMER ON THE PRAIRIE
by Henryk Sienkiewicz

HENRYK SIENKIEWICZ, author of the Nobel-prize-winning novel *Quo Vadis?*, was poor and unknown when he came to America in 1876 on an assignment to write travel articles for a Polish newspaper. His real purpose for undertaking the trip, however, was quite a different one. Together with the famous actress, Madame Modjeska, and some other Polish friends, Sienkiewicz wanted to found a sort of utopian farm community. After traveling across the whole of the United States, he decided that Anaheim in Southern California would make an excellent site for the experiment in "togetherness." The friends arrived the following year but unfortunately, although they were idealistic and high-minded, they lacked any practical sense. As a result the experiment in group living was a failure, and Sienkiewicz went home to his native Poland where he wrote a trilogy that was full of the hope, the optimism, and the belief in the future which had seemed to him characteristic of America.

The picture of summer on the American prairies was observed from a train window crossing Nebraska.

Only in the evening when the great red orb of the sun begins to vanish below the horizon does the prairie come to life. Here and there are heard the angry, throaty screams of the jaguars. Sometimes an old grey bear roars in reply. Then for a moment everything falls silent. Later the breeze carries the plaintive whine of the coyotes, the small prairie wolves that follow in the tracks of the great marauders and live off the remnants of the feast.

Most of the animal life is found near the rivers and lakes whose waters do not dry up despite the heat. Hidden in the reeds and rushes along the shores is a whole menagerie of animals. Against the red rays of the setting sun are outlined with strange clarity the immense, black silhouettes of the buffaloes. They are coming at a trot over the high prairies toward the water. Into it they plunge joyously head and all. With light, graceful leaps, small herds of picturesque antelope approach and after them crawl stealthily the beasts of prey. Occasionally the grass and bushes are parted and for a moment an Indian's head, decorated with feathers, appears. Squatting low on his horse and armed with a javelin, the red warrior scans with glowing eyes these creatures soon to become his victims.

During the hours of intense heat when everything on the prairie is silent and asleep and when even the Indian seeks refuge in the shade of his tepee, only one creature dares to expose his head to the sun's rays and that creature is the white man. Often when the temperature is at its highest and the air is filled with dust, you will see huge wagons, here called "prairie schooners," drawn by three, four and even six pairs of mules. The ring and clatter of such a caravan can be heard from afar, for to each mule's collar four bells are attached whose sound urges the animals on and gives them added strength. The tops of the wagons are covered with striped canvas, and inside are the women, children, and household belongings. Behind the caravan trail herds of cattle and sheep, often driven by Negroes or Mestizos who crack their long whips and shout "Ho! Ho!" or curse the heat and each other. Alongside of each team a man walks slowly, dressed in a flannel shirt, wearing a huge sombrero to protect him from the sun.

They are settlers headed for the Far West. Frequently they themselves do not know where they are going. Sometimes they are able to cite a state or territory. "We are going to Kansas, Colorado, or Nebraska," they say, "or else into the silent prairie. When we find land, some trees and water, there we shall settle."

1879

THE EMIGRANT TRAIN
by Robert Louis Stevenson

ROBERT LOUIS STEVENSON came to America in 1879 to be with his fiancée, Fanny Osbourne, who was in San Francisco waiting to get a divorce from her husband. Stevenson was impoverished and in poor health, but he was too proud to ask his strait-laced Calvinist parents to pay for the trip. They were certain to disapprove of his marrying a woman some years older than he and a divorcée.

Against the advice of his friends, Stevenson, with his usual courage and gallantry, ignored his poor health and embarked on the long journey, traveling across the Atlantic in the steerage and boarding an emigrant train in New York to save money.

The trip in the emigrant train nearly cost him his life; but Stevenson's spirits never wavered. "No man is any use until he has dared everything," he wrote a friend from the crowded train which took eleven days to cross the continent. "I feel just now as if I had, and so might become a man."

In spite of these brave words, the hardships which he suffered on the journey made him desperately ill. In San Francisco he collapsed with galloping consumption. Fanny Osbourne succeeded in nursing him back to a precarious half-health, but Stevenson was never able to live a normal life again. In *The Amateur Emigrant,* he describes his trip in the emigrant train.

It was about two in the afternoon of Friday (1879) that I found myself in front of the Emigrant House, with more than a hundred others to be sorted and boxed for the journey. A white-haired official, with a stick under one arm, and a list in the other hand, stood apart in front of us, and called name after name in a tone of command. At each name you would see a family gather up its brats and bundles and run for the hindmost of the three cars that stood awaiting us, and I soon concluded that this was to be set apart for the women and children. The second or central car, it turned out, was devoted to men travelling alone, and the third to the Chinese.

The families once housed, we men carried the second car without ceremony by simultaneous assault. I suppose the reader has some notion of an American railroad-car, that long, narrow wooden box, like a flat-roofed Noah's ark, with a stove and a convenience, one at either end, a passage down the middle, and transverse benches upon either hand. Those destined for emigrants on the Union Pacific are only remarkable for their extreme plainness, nothing but wood entering into any part of their constitution, and for the usual inefficacy of the lamps, which often went out and shed but a dying glimmer even while they burned. The benches are too short for anything but a young child. Where there is scarce elbow-room for two to sit, there will not be space enough for one to lie. Hence the company, or rather the company's servants, have conceived a plan for the better accommodation of travellers. They prevail on every two to chum together. To each of the chums they sell a board and three square cushions stuffed with straw, and covered with thin cotton. The benches can be made to face each other in pairs, for the backs are reversible. On the approach of night the boards are laid from bench to bench, making a couch wide enough for two, and long enough for a man of the middle height; and the chums lie down side by side upon the cushions with the head to the conductor's van and the feet to the engine. The price for one board and three straw cushions began with two dollars and a half; but before the train left, and, I am sorry to say, long after I had purchased mine, it had fallen to one dollar and a half.

At last about six, the long train crawled out of Transfer Station (Council Bluffs, Missouri) and across the wide Missouri river to Omaha, westward bound. The day faded; the lamps were lit; a party of wild young men, who got off next evening at North Platte, stood together on the stern platform, singing "The Sweet Bye-and-bye" with very tuneful voices; the chums began to put up their beds; and it seemed as if the business of the day were at an end. But it was not so; for the train stopping at some station, the cars were instantly thronged with the natives, wives and fathers, young men and maidens, some of them in little more than nightgear, some with stable lanterns, and all offering beds for sale. Their charge began with twenty-five cents a cushion, but fell before the train went on again, to fifteen, with the bed-board gratis, or less than one-fifth of what I had paid at the Transfer.

A great personage on an American train is the news-boy. He sells books (such books!), papers, fruit, lollipops, and cigars; and on emigrant journeys, soap, towels, tin washing dishes, tin coffee pitchers, coffee, tea, sugar, and tinned eatables, mostly hash or beans and bacon. Early next morning the newsboy went around the cars, and chumming on a more extended principle became the order of the hour. It requires but a copartnery of two to manage beds; but washing and eating can be carried on most economically by a syndicate of three. I myself entered a little after sunrise into articles of agreement,

139

and became one of the firm of Pennsylvania, Shakespeare, and Dubuque. Shakespeare was my own nickname on the cars; Pennsylvania that of my bedfellow; and Dubuque, that of an amiable young fellow going west to cure an asthma, and retarding his recovery by incessantly chewing or smoking tobacco, and sometimes chewing and smoking together. Shakespeare bought a tin washing-dish, Dubuque a towel, and Pennsylvania a brick of soap. The partners used these instruments, one after another, according to the order of their first awaking; and when the firm had finished there was no want of borrowers. Each filled the tin dish at the water filter opposite the stove, and retired with the whole stock in trade to the platform of the car. There he knelt down, supporting himself by a shoulder against the woodwork or one elbow crooked about the railing, and made a shift to wash his face and neck and hands: a cold, an insufficient, and, if the train is moving rapidly, a somewhat dangerous toilet.

On a similar division of expense, the firm of Pennsylvania, Shakespeare, and Dubuque supplied themselves with coffee, sugar, and necessary vessels. Before the sun was up the stove would be brightly burning; at the first station the natives would come on board with milk and eggs and coffee cakes; and soon from end to end the car would be filled with little parties breakfasting upon the bed-boards.

I had been suffering in my health a good deal all the way; and at last, whether I was exhausted by my complaint or poisoned, the evening we left Laramie, I fell sick outright. That was a night which I shall not readily forget. The lamps did not go out; each made a faint shining in its own neighborhood, and the shadows were confounded together in the long, hollow box of the car. The sleepers lay in uneasy attitudes; here two chums alongside, flat upon their backs like dead folk; there a man sprawling on the floor, with his face upon his arm; there another half seated with his head and shoulders on the bench. The most passive were continually and roughly shaken by the movement of the train; others stirred, turned, or stretched out their arms like children; it was surprising how many groaned and murmured in their sleep. Although it was chill, I was obliged to open my window, for the degradation of the air soon became intolerable to one who was awake and using the full supply of life. Outside, in a glimmering night, I saw the black, amorphous hills shoot by unweariedly in our wake. They that long for morning have never longed for it more earnestly than I.

1883

THE AMERICAN NEWSPAPER
by Matthew Arnold

MATTHEW ARNOLD came to the United States in 1883 to give a series of lectures. Just past sixty, he was at the height of his fame as a poet, a writer of prose works and as a former Professor of Poetry at Oxford.

In most cities he drew large audiences, although as he moved into the Midwest he attracted smaller groups. From a financial point of view in any case, his tour was a success. Back in England, he published his *Discourses in America* (1885) and, in the last year of his life, his famous *Civilization in the United States,* from which the following excerpt has been taken.

It is often said that every nation has the government it deserves. What is much more certain is that every nation has the newspapers it deserves. The newspaper is the direct product of the want felt; the supply answers closely and inevitably to the demand. I suppose no one knows what the American newspapers are, who has not been obliged, for some length of time, to read either those newspapers or none at all. Powerful and valuable contributions occur scattered about in them. But on the whole, and taking the total impression and effect made by them, I should say that if one were searching for the best means to efface and kill in a whole nation the discipline of respect, the feeling for what is elevated, one could not do better than take the American newspapers. The absence of truth and soberness in them, the poverty in serious interest, the personality and sensation-mongering are beyond belief. There are a few newspapers which are in whole, or in part, exceptions.

The Americans used to say to me that what they valued was news, and that this their newspapers gave them. I at last made the reply: "Yes, news for the servants' hall!" I remember that a New York newspaper, one of the first I saw after landing in the country, had a long account, with the prominence we should give to the illness of the German Emperor or the arrest of the Lord Mayor of Dublin, of a young woman who had married a man who was a bag of bones, as we say, and who used to exhibit himself as a skeleton; of her growing horror in living with this man, and finally of her death. All this in the most intimate detail, and described with all the writer's power of rhetoric. This has always remained by me as a specimen of what the Americans call news.

You must have lived amongst their newspapers to know what they are. If I relate some of my own experiences, it is because these will give a clear enough notion of what the newspapers over there are, and one remembers more definitely what has happened to oneself. Soon after arriving in Boston, I opened a Boston newspaper and came upon a column headed: "Tickings." By *tickings* we are to understand news conveyed through the tickings of the telegraph. The first "ticking" was: "Matthew Arnold is sixty-two years old"—an age, I must just say in passing, which I had not then reached. The second "ticking" was: "Wales says, Mary is a darling," the meaning being that the Prince of Wales expressed great admiration for Miss

Mary Anderson [a prominent actress of the day]. I proceeded to Chicago. An evening paper was given me soon after I arrived; I opened it, and found under a large-type heading, *"We have seen him arrive,"* the following picture of myself: "He has harsh features, supercilious manners, parts his hair down the middle, wears a single eye-glass and ill-fitting clothes." Notwithstanding this rather unfavorable introduction, I was most kindly and hospitably received at Chicago.

It happened that I had a letter for Mr. Medill, an elderly gentleman of Scotch descent, the editor of the chief newspaper in those parts, the *Chicago Tribune.* I called on him, and we conversed amiably together. Some time afterwards, when I had gone back to England, a New York paper published a criticism of Chicago and its people, purporting to have been contributed by me to the *Pall Mall Gazette* over here. It was a poor hoax, but many people were taken in and were excusably angry. Mr. Medill of the *Chicago Tribune* amongst the number. A friend telegraphed to me to know if I had written the criticism. I, of course, instantly telegraphed back that I had not written a syllable of it. Then a Chicago paper is sent to me; and what I have the pleasure of reading, as the result of my contradiction, is this: "Arnold denies; Mr. Medill (my old friend) refuses to accept Arnold's disclaimer; says Arnold is a cur."

What really dissatisfies in American civilization is the want of the *interesting*, a want due chiefly to the want of those two great elements of the interesting, which are elevation and beauty. And it seems to me that what the Americans now most urgently require [is] a steady exhibition of cool and sane criticism by their men of light and leading over there. And perhaps the very first step of such men should be to insist on having for America, and to create if need be, better newspapers.

A VISIT TO WALT WHITMAN

by Edmund Gosse

EDMUND GOSSE, one of England's most distinguished critics and editors, was not an admirer of Whitman's poetry and had not planned to visit the poet when he came to the United States in the winter of 1884. It was Whitman who sought the interview. "I received a note from Whitman," Gosse says, "asking me not to leave America without seeing him. My first instinct was promptly to decline the invitation. Camden, New Jersey, was a very long way off. But better counsel prevailed; curiosity and civility combined to draw me, and I wrote to him that I would come. It would be fatuous to mention all this, if it were not that I particularly wish to bring out the peculiar magic of the old man, acting, not on a disciple, but on a stiff-necked and forward unbeliever."

In his report of the interview with the old poet, Gosse succeeds in catching the "magic" of Whitman's personality, so that one is not surprised when Gosse sums up the encounter: "And so an unbeliever went to see Walt Whitman and was captivated without being converted."

I started early on the 3d [January], crossed the broad Delaware River, where blocks of ice bumped and cracked around us. I was put ashore in a crude and apparently uninhabited village, grim with that concentrated ugliness that only an American township in the depth of winter can display. I wandered aimlessly about, and was just ready to give all I possessed to be back again in New York, when I discovered that I was opposite No. 328 Mickle Street, and that on a minute brass plate was engraved "W. Whitman." I knocked at this dreary little two-story tenement house, and wondered what was going to happen. A melancholy woman opened the door. Before I could speak, a large figure, hobbling down the stairs, called out in a cheery voice, "Is that my friend?" Suddenly, by I know not what magnetic charm, all wire-drawn literary reservations faded out of being, and one's only sensation was of gratified satisfaction at being the "friend" of this very nice old gentleman.

There was a good deal of greeting on the stairs, and then the host, moving actively, though clumsily, and with a stick, advanced to his own dwelling-room on the first story. The opening impression was, as the closing one would be, of extreme simplicity. A large room, without carpet on the scrubbed planks, a small bedstead, a little round stove with a stack-pipe in the middle of the room, one chair—that was all the furniture. On the walls and in the fireplace such a miserable wall-paper—tinted, with a spot—as one sees in the bedrooms of labourers' cottages; no pictures hung in the room, but pegs and shelves loaded with objects. Various boxes lay about, and one huge clamped trunk, and heaps, mountains of papers in a wild confusion, swept up here and there into stacks and peaks; but all the room, and the old man himself clean in the highest degree, raised to the nth power of stainlessness, scoured and scrubbed to such a pitch that dirt seemed defied for all remaining time. Whitman, in particular, in his suit of hodden grey and shirt thrown wide open at the throat, his grey hair and whiter beard voluminously flowing, seemed positively blanched with cleanliness; the whole man sand-white with spotlessness, like a deal table that has grown old under the scrubbing-brush.

Whitman sat down in the one chair with a small poker in his hand and spent much of his leisure in feeding and irritating the stove. When he was not actively engaged upon the stove his steady attention was fixed upon his visitor. He sat with a very curious pose of the head thrown backward, as if resting it one vertebra lower down the spinal column than other people do, and thus tilting his face a little upward. With his head so poised and the whole man fixed in contemplation of the interlocutor, he seemed to pass into a state of absolute passivity, waiting for remarks or incidents, the

145

glassy eyes half-closed, the large knotted hands spread out before him. So he would remain, immovable for a quarter of an hour at a time, even the action of speech betraying no movement, the lips hidden under a cascade of beard.

His talk was elemental, like his writings. It had none of the usual ornaments or irritants of conversation. It welled out naturally, or stopped; it was innocent of every species of rhetoric or epigram. Whitman sat there with his great head tilted back, smiling serenely, and he talked about himself. He mentioned his poverty, which was patent, and his paralysis; those were the two burdens beneath which he crouched, like Issachar; he seemed to be quite at home with both of them, and scarcely heeded them. I think I asked leave to move my box, for the light began to pour in at the great uncurtained window; and then Whitman said that some one had promised him a gift of curtains, but he was not eager for them, he thought they "kept out some of the light." Light and air, that was all he wanted; and through the winter he sat there patiently waiting for the air and light of summer, when he would hobble out again and bask his body in a shallow creek he knew "back at Camden." Meanwhile he waited, waited with infinite patience, uncomplaining, thinking about the sand and the thin hot layer of water over it, in that shy New Jersey creek.

In the bareness of Whitman's great double room only two objects suggested art in any way. One was a print of a Red Indian; it had inspired the passage about "the red aborigines" in *Staring from Paumanok*. The other—positively the sole and only thing that redeemed the bareness of the back-room where Whitman's bound works were stored—was a photograph of a very handsome young man in a boat, sculling. I asked him about this portrait and he said several notable things in consequence. He explained, first of all, that this was one of his greatest friends, a professional oarsman from Canada, a well-known sporting character. He continued, that these were the people he liked best, athletes who had a business in the open air;

that those were the plainest and most affectionate of men, those who lived in the light and air and had to study to keep their bodies clean and fresh and ruddy; that his soul went out to such people. "And now," he went on, "I only wait for the spring, to hobble out with my staff into the woods, and when I can sit all day long close to a set of woodmen at their work, I am perfectly happy, for something of their life mixes with the smell of the chopped timber, and it passes into my veins and I am old and ill no longer."

It might be supposed, and I think that even admirers have said, that Whitman had no humour. But that seemed to me not quite correct. No boisterous humour, truly, but a gentle sort of sly fun. For example, he told me of some tribute from India, and added, with a twinkling smile, "You see, 'I sound my barbaric yawp over the roofs of the world.' " But this was rare: mostly he seemed dwelling in a vague pastoral life, the lovely days when he was young.

As I passed from the little house and stood in dull, deserted Mickle Street once more, my heart was full of affection for this beautiful old man, who had just said in his calm accents, "Goodbye, my friend!" I felt that the experience of the day was embalmed by something that a great poet [Shelley] had written long ago:

> Peace within and calm around,
> And that content, surpassing wealth,
> The sage in meditation found,
> And walk'd with inward glory crown'd.

RANCH LIFE AND THE COMING OF "PROSPERITY"

by Horace Annesley Vachell

H. A. VACHELL came to America in the early 1880's with his brother to live the rough, outdoor, adventurous life of a rancher. He married an American and they settled down on a ranch in Southern California. But when, seventeen years later, prosperity caught up with them and the old pioneering ranch life gave way to a tamer civilization, Vachell gave up and went home to his native England.

The writers who have described ranch-life as easy and leisurely, have —consciously or unconsciously—lied.

On a cattle-ranch you will be sensible of its remoteness. You are far from railroad and post-office. Once a week, perhaps, you get papers and letters. You rise early, feed your horse and yourself, and ride forth into the hills. After a time you begin to know your cattle; you can see them, distinguish one from another at a distance that surprises a tenderfoot. If one is missing you are aware instinctively of the fact, and glance skyward. A buzzard circling slowly on motionless pinions advises you that the beast is dead or dying. Perhaps he has mired down in some rotten ground, or is cast in a gulch, or stolen. It is the business of your life to know where the cattle are, and what may be their condition. At certain seasons the calves must be branded; the estrays must be given to their lawful owners. These *rodeos* are the high days, not the holidays, of ranch life. From the neighboring ranches ride the cowboys, and in the corrals you will see them at work with the lasso and the branding iron. Time was when cattle were roughly handled. They came streaming across the hills, the vaqueros shouting behind them and whirling their *reatas*.

Now quieter methods prevail. The foreman instructs his men to drive the beasts slowly, *not* to shout, *not* to swing the *reata*. He wants his cattle tame. Even in the corral the lasso is less used than formerly, and the skill of the vaqueros is passing for lack of practise. Some of the "greasers," however, can still fling a rope with such exquisite art that the loop seems to be guided by an invisible hand to the horn or hoof it is destined to encircle; they can vault on, and off, and over a horse at full gallop, or snatch a coin from the ground as they race by—swinging far out of their big saddles and into them again with extraordinary grace and agility; they can "tail" a bull; they can "tie up" and *untie* a wild Texan steer, single-handed; and they can break and ride anything that goes on all fours. In the days before the American occupation of the Pacific Slope the mastery of such feats was part, the larger part, of a *caballero's* education, and the vaquero was held in high esteem. To-day, poor fellow, his occupation is almost gone.

In '86 the rise in the value of land, with increased taxation and a fall in the price of cattle, turned many rancheros into farmers. The big Spanish grants were cut up and sold in small tracts to Eastern and mid-Western buyers. These men fenced their farms with barbed wire, built ramshackle board-and-batten houses and barns, and talked glibly of *improvements*. In an incredibly short time, the superb trees—the live oaks, white oaks, madrones, sycamores, and cotton woods—were chopped down. A spirit of utilitarianism was abroad, smiting hip and thigh, sparing nothing, not even the ancient mission of San Luis Obispo. It stands to-day smugly respectable in a cheap modern overcoat of concrete and paint. The picturesque tiles have been thrown to the void; the pillars and arches have been pulled down; and the padre's garden—a cool sequestered pleasance, fragrant with herbs whose very names and uses are forgotten—has been subdivided into town lots!

Once upon the steps of the church, I met an old Spanish woman, whose withered face was framed in a soft black shawl, most becomingly draped. She chattered of the pleasant yesterdays, and I asked idly if she approved the changes that had been wrought in the ancient building.

"My American friends," she answered in her own tongue, "tell me to wear a jacket with big sleeves, and to buy a bonnet, but, *senor*, this shawl suits me best. And the Mission was getting like me—ugly and wrinkled; but I wish they had left it—its old shawl."

My brother and I sold our cattle, and began to sow wheat in our valley and on our hills. Some of the neighbors planted out large orchards and vineyards; others opened stores. Churches and school-houses were built. Everywhere, even in the brush hills, was heard the buzz of the big threshing machines, the skirl of the circular saws, the clang of the hammer and anvil; all the sounds, in fine, of what is called Prosperity.

1889

THE BEND

by Jacob Riis

In 1870 JACOB RIIS, a young Danish emigrant who had just finished his apprenticeship to a carpenter, sailed for America in the steerage to seek his fortune. "I had a pair of strong hands," he writes, "and stubbornness to do for two; also a strong belief in a free country, free from the domination of custom, of caste, as well as of men."

After a rough start in which he tried his luck unsuccessfully at a variety of odd jobs which ranged all the way from selling flat-irons to working in a coal mine, he found the "corner where he belonged," as a newspaper reporter. Co-operating with the Health Department and the police, he fought with dedication, compassion and a "consecrated pen" to improve the lot of other poor emigrants who, like himself, had come "with little cash but high hopes to seek a better life in a young and free country."

Where Mulberry Street crooks like an elbow within hail of the old depravity of the Five Points, is "the Bend," foul core of New York's slums. Long years ago the cows coming home from the pasture trod a path over this hill. Echoes of tinkling bells linger there still, but they do not call up memories of green meadows; they proclaim the home-coming of the rag-picker's cart. Around "the Bend" cluster the bulk of the tenements that are stamped as altogether bad, even by the optimists of the Health Department. Incessant raids cannot keep down the crowds that make them their home. In the scores of back alleys, of stable lanes and hidden byways, of which the rent collector alone can keep track, they share such shelter as the ramshackle structures afford with every kind of abomination rifled from the dumps and ash-barrels of the city. Here, too, shunning the light, skulks the unclean beast of dishonest idleness. "The Bend" is the home of the tramp as well as the rag-picker.

The whole district is a maze of narrow, often unsuspected passage-ways—necessarily, for there is scarce a lot that has not two, three, or four tenements upon it, swarming with unwholesome crowds. What a bird's-eye view of "the Bend" would be like is a matter of bewildering conjecture. Its everyday appearance, as seen from the corner of Bayard Street on a sunny day, is one of the sights of New York.

Bayard Street is the high road to Jewtown across the Bowery, picketed from end to end with the outposts of Israel. Hebrew faces, Hebrew signs, and incessant chatter in the queer lingo that passes for Hebrew on the East Side attend the curious wanderer to the very corner of Mulberry Street. But the moment he turns the corner the scene changes abruptly. Before him lies spread out what might better be the market-place in some town in Southern Italy than a street in New York—all but the houses; they are still the same old tenements. When the sun shines the entire population seeks the street, carrying on its household work, its bargaining, its love-making on street or sidewalk, or idling there when it has nothing better to do, with the reverse of the impulse that makes the Polish Jew coop himself up in his den with the thermometer at stewing heat. Along the curb women sit in rows, young and old alike, with the odd head covering, pad or turban, haggling over baskets of frowsy weeds, some sort of salad probably, stale tomatoes, and oranges not above suspicion. Ash-barrels serve them as counters, and not infrequently does the arrival of the official cart en route for the dump cause a temporary suspension of trade until the barrels have been emptied and restored. Hucksters and pedlars' carts make two rows of booths in the street itself, and along the houses is still an-other—a perpetual market doing a very lively trade in its own queer staples, found nowhere on American ground save in "the Bend."

Abuse is the normal condition of "the Bend," murder its every-day crop, with the tenants not always the criminals. In this block between Bayard, Park, Mulberry and Baxter Streets, "the Bend" proper, the late Tenement House Commission counted 155 deaths of children in a specimen year (1882). The infant mortality of any city or place as compared with the whole number of deaths is justly considered a good barometer of its general sanitary condition. Here, in this tenement, No. 59½, next to Bandit's Roost, fourteen persons died that year, and eleven of them were children; in No. 61 eleven, and eight of them not yet five years old. These figures speak for themselves, when it is shown that in the model tenement across the way at Nos. 48 and 50, where the same class of people live in greater swarms (161 according to the record) but under good management, and in decent quarters, the hearse called that year only twice for a baby.

Bottle Alley is around the corner in Baxter Street; but it is a fair specimen of its kind, wherever found. Look into any of these houses, everywhere the same piles of rags, of malodorous bones and musty paper. Here is a "flat" of "parlor" and two pitch-dark coops called bedrooms. Truly, the bed is all there is room for. The family tea-kettle is on the stove, doing duty for the time being as a wash-boiler. By night it will have returned to its proper use again, a practical illustration of how poverty in "the Bend" makes both ends meet. One, two, three beds are there, if the old boxes and heaps of foul straw can be called by that name; a broken stove with a crazy pipe from which the smoke leaks at every joint, a table of rough boards propped up on boxes, piles of rubbish in the corner. The closeness and smell are appalling.

What squalor and degradation inhabit these dens the health officers know. Through the long summer days their carts patrol "the Bend," scattering disinfectants in streets and lanes, in sinks and cellars, and hidden hovels where the tramp burrows. From midnight till far into the small hours of the morning the policeman's thundering rap on closed doors is heard, on his rounds gathering evidence of illegal over-crowding. In a room not thirteen feet either way slept twelve men and women, two or three in bunks set in a sort of alcove, the rest on the floor. A kerosine lamp burned dimly in the fearful atmosphere, probably to guide other and later arrivals to their "bed." A baby's fretful wail came from an adjoining hall-room, where, in the semi-darkness, three recumbent figures could be made out. The "apartment" was one of three in two adjoining buildings we had found, within half an hour, similarly crowded. Most of the men were lodgers, who slept there for five cents a spot.

Another room on the top floor, that had been examined a few

nights before was comparatively empty. The landlord opened the door with alacrity. Our visit had been anticipated. The policeman's back was probably no sooner turned than the room was reopened for business.

1889

SAN FRANCISCO IMPRESSIONS
by Rudyard Kipling

RUDYARD KIPLING was a young man of twenty-three when he landed in San Francisco in 1889 on his way home from India to England. He was not yet famous but had already published some poems and a book of stories and sketches, *Plain Tales from the Hills.*

Kipling came back to America in 1892 after he had married an American girl, Caroline Balestier. They settled in her home town, Brattleboro, Vermont, where Kipling wrote both the "Jungle Books" and *Captains Courageous.* A quarrel with his brother-in-law sent Kipling back to England where he lived until his death, growing more and more famous as a poet, a teller of tales, and as the champion of the British Empire. Kipling won the Nobel Prize for Literature in 1907.

The American of wealth is owned by his family. They exploit him for bullion, and sometimes it seems to me that his lot is a lonely one. The women get the ha'pence; the kicks are all his own. Nothing is too good for an American's daughter (I speak here of the moneyed classes). The girls take every gift as a matter of course. Yet they develop greatly when a catastrophe arrives and the man of many millions goes up or goes down and his daughters take to stenography or type-writing. I have heard many tales of heroism from the lips of girls who counted the principals among their friends. The crash came; Mamie or Hattie or Sadie gave up their maid, their carriages and candy, and with a No. 2 Remington and a stout heart set about earning their daily bread.

"And did I drop her from the list of my friends? No, Sir," said a scarlet-lipped vision in white lace. "That might happen to me any day."

It may be this sense of possible disaster in the air that makes San Francisco society go with so captivating a rush and whirl. Recklessness is in the air. The roaring winds of the Pacific make you drunk to begin with. The aggressive luxury on all sides helps out the intoxication, and you spin for ever "down the ringing groves of change" (there is no small change, by the way, west of the Rockies) as long as money lasts. They make greatly and they spend lavishly; not only the rich but the artisans, who pay nearly five pounds [$25] for a suit of clothes and for other luxuries in proportion.

The young men rejoice in the days of their youth. They gamble, yacht, race, enjoy prize-fights and cock-fights—the one openly, the other in secret—they establish luxurious clubs; they break themselves over horse-flesh; and they are in instant quarrel. At twenty they are experienced in business; embark in vast enterprises, take partners as experienced as themselves, and go to pieces with as much splendour as their neighbors. Remember that the men who stocked California in the Fifties were physically, and as far as regards certain tough virtues, the pick of the earth. The inept and the weakly died *en route* or went under in the days of construction. To this nucleus were added all the races of the Continent—French, Italian, German and Jew. The result you shall see in large-boned, deep-chested, delicate-handed women, and long, elastic, well-built boys. It needs no little golden badge swinging from his watch-chain to mark the Native Son of the Golden West—the country-bred of

155

California. Him I love because he is devoid of fear, carries himself like a man, and has a heart as big as his boots.

The tale of the resources of California—vegetable and mineral—is a fairy-tale. You can read it in books. You would never believe me. All manner of nourishing food from sea-fish to beef may be bought at the lowest prices; and the people are well developed and of a high stomach. They demand ten shillings [$2.50] for tinkering a jammed lock of a trunk; they receive sixteen shillings [$4] a day for working as carpenters; they spend many six-pences on very bad cigars, and they go mad over a prize-fight. When they disagree, they do so fatally, with firearms in their hands, and on the public streets.

I was just clear of Mission Street when the trouble began between two gentlemen, one of whom perforated the other. When a policeman, whose name I do not recollect, "fatally shot Ed. Kearney," for attempting to escape arrest, I was in the next street. For these I am thankful. It is enough to travel with a policeman in a tram-car, and while he arranges his coattails as he sits down, to catch sight of a loaded revolver. It is enough to know that fifty per cent of the men in public saloons carry pistols about them. The Chinaman waylays his adversary and methodically chops him to pieces with his hatchet. Then the Press roars about the brutal ferocity of the Pagan. The Italian reconstructs his friend with a long knife. The Press complains of the waywardness of the alien. The Irishman and the native Californian in their hours of discontent use the revolver, not once, but six times. The Press records the fact, and asks in the next column whether the world can parallel the progress of San Francisco.

1889

AN INTERVIEW WITH MARK TWAIN
by Rudyard Kipling

KIPLING'S INTERVIEW with Mark Twain, in Elmira, New York, is interesting not only because of the picture it gives us of the famous American writer; it is fascinating also as a self-portrait of an eager young journalist with an eye for the revealing gesture and an ear for the significant word—assets that were to make him one of the best-loved storytellers of all time.

A big, darkened drawing-room; a huge chair; a man with eyes, a mane of grizzled hair, a brown mustache covering a mouth as delicate as a woman's, a strong, square hand shaking mine, and the slowest, calmest, levellest voice in all the world saying:—

"Well, you think you owe me something, and you've come to tell me so. That's what I call squaring a debt handsomely."

"Piff!" from a cob-pipe and, behold! Mark Twain had curled himself up in the big arm-chair, and I was smoking reverently, as befits one in the presence of his superior.

The thing that struck me first was that he was an elderly man; yet, after a minute's thought, I perceived that it was otherwise, and in five minutes, the eyes looking at me, I saw that the grey hair was an accident of the most trivial. He was quite young.

Growing bold, and feeling that I had a few hundred thousand folk at my back, I demanded whether Tom Sawyer married Judge Thatcher's daughter and whether we were ever going to hear of Tom Sawyer as a man.

"I haven't decided," quoth Mark Twain, getting up, filling his pipe, and walking up and down the room in his slippers. "I have a notion of writing the sequel to *Tom Sawyer* in two ways. In one I

157

would make him rise to great honour and go to Congress, and in the other I should hang him. Then the friends and enemies of the book could take their choice."

Here I lost my reverence completely, and protested against any theory of the sort, because, to me at least, Tom Sawyer was real.

"Oh, he *is* real," said Mark Twain. "He's all the boy that I have known or recollect."

Returning to the big chair, he, speaking of truth and the like in literature, said that an autobiography was the one work in which a man, against his own will and in spite of his utmost striving to the contrary, revealed himself in his true light to the world.

"A good deal of your life on the Mississippi is autobiographical, isn't it?" I asked.

"As near as it can be—when a man is writing to a book and about himself."

"Do you ever intend to write an autobiography?"

"If I do, it will be as other men have done—with the most earnest desire to make myself out to be the better man in every little business that has been to my discredit; and I shall fail, like the others, to make my readers believe anything except the truth."

Here he told me a little—such things as a man may tell a stranger —of his early life and upbringing, and in what manner he had been influenced for good by the example of his parents. He spoke always through his eyes, a light under the heavy eyebrows; anon crossing the room with a step as light as a girl's, to show me some book or other; then resuming his walk up and down the room, puffing at the cob pipe.

He recurled himself into the chair and talked of other things.

"I spend nine months of the year at Hartford. I have long ago satisfied myself that there is no hope of doing much work during those nine months. People come in and call. They call at all hours, about everything in the world. I come here for three months every year, and I work for four or five hours a day in a study down the garden of the little house on the hill. Of course, I do not object to two or three interruptions. When a man is in the full swing of his work these little things do not affect him. Eight or ten or twenty interruptions retard composition."

I was burning to ask him all manner of impertinent questions, as to which of his works he preferred, and so forth, but, standing in awe of his eyes, I dared not. He spoke on.

It was a question of mental equipment that was on the carpet, and I am still wondering whether he meant what he said.

"Personally I never care for fiction or story-books. What I like to read about are facts and statistics of any kind. If they are only facts about the raising of radishes, they interest me. Just now, for instance, I was reading an article about 'Mathematics.' Perfectly pure Mathematics.

"I didn't understand a word of it; but facts, or what a man believes to be facts, are always delightful. That mathematical fellow believed in his facts. So do I. Get your facts first, and"—the voice dies away to an almost inaudible drone—"then you can distort 'em as much as you please."

Bearing this precious advice in my bosom, I left; the great man assuring me with gentle kindness that I had not interrupted him in the least.

1893

From THE PROMISED LAND
by Mary Antin

BORN IN Polotzk, Russia, a place that was divided into two separate
worlds, that of the Jew and that of the Gentile, Mary Antin was
taken from her ghetto and brought to America by her emigrant
father in 1893. To the little Jewish girl who had been harassed
and discriminated against all her life long, America was the
"Promised Land." In the Russia of those days, Jewish children could
enter high school only in the ratio of ten to a hundred and then
only after taking special examinations in which a Jewish child
of nine had to answer questions a thirteen-year-old Gentile child
could hardly be expected to understand; so that the free American
school system was to Mary Antin a symbol of the democracy she had
always longed for and been denied.

In America, then, everything was free, as we had heard in Russia.
Light was free; the streets were as bright as a synagogue on a holy
day. Music was free; we had been serenaded, to our gaping delight,
by a brass band of many pieces, soon after our installation on Union
Place.

Education was free. That subject my father had written about
repeatedly, as comprising his chief hope for us children, the essence
of American opportunity, the treasure that no thief could touch, not
even misfortune or poverty. It was the one thing that he was able to
promise us when he sent for us; surer, safer than bread or shelter. On
our second day I was thrilled with the realization of what this freedom of education meant. A little girl from across the alley came and
offered to conduct us to school. My father was out, but we five
between us had a few words of English by this time. We knew the
word school. We understood. This child, who had never seen us till
yesterday, who could not pronounce our names, who was not much

better dressed than we, was able to offer us the freedom of the schools of Boston! No application made, no questions asked, no examinations, rulings, exclusions; no machinations, no fees. The doors stood open for every one of us. The smallest child could show us the way.

This incident impressed me more than anything I had heard in advance of the freedom of education in America. It was a concrete proof—almost the thing itself. One had to experience it to understand it.

Father himself conducted us to school. He would not have delegated that mission to the President of the United States. He had awaited the day with impatience equal to mine. If education, culture, the higher life were shining things to be worshipped from afar, he had still a means left whereby he could draw one step nearer to them. He could send his children to school, to learn all those things that he knew by fame to be desirable.

So it was with a heart full of longing and hope that my father led us to school on that first day. He took long strides in his eagerness, the rest of us running and hopping to keep up.

At last the four of us stood around the teacher's desk; and my father, in his impossible English, gave us over in her charge, with some broken word of his hopes for us that his swelling heart could no longer contain. I venture to say that Miss Nixon was struck by something uncommon in the group we made. My little sister was as pretty as a doll, with her clear pink-and-white face, short golden curls, and eyes like blue violets when you caught them looking up. My brother might have been a girl, too, with his cherubic contours of face, rich red color, glossy black hair and fine eye-brows. Whatever secret fears were in his heart, remembering his former teachers, who had taught with the rod, he stood up straight and uncringing before the American teacher, his cap respectfully doffed. Next to him stood a starved-looking girl with eyes ready to pop out, and short dark curls that would not have made much of a wig for a Jewish bride.

All three children carried themselves rather better than the common run of "green" pupils that were brought to Miss Nixon. But the figure that challenged attention to the group was the tall, straight father, with his earnest face and fine forehead, nervous hands eloquent in gesture, and a voice full of feeling. This foreigner, who brought his children to school as if it were an act of consecration, who regarded the teacher of the primer class with reverence, who spoke of visions, like a man inspired, in a common schoolroom, was not like other aliens, who brought their children in dull obedience to the law; was not like native fathers, who brought their unmanageable boys, glad to be relieved of their care. I think Miss Nixon guessed what my father's best English could not convey. I think she divined that by the simple act of delivering our school certificates to her he took possession of America.

Bibliography

The extracts included in this book may be found in the following sources:

Pages 4 and 6. *Chronicles of the Pilgrim Fathers from 1602–1605,* by Alexander Young. Boston: Little, Brown & Co., 1841.

Page 9. *A Narration of the Indian Wars in New England from the First Planting Thereof in the Year 1667 to the Year 1677,* by William Hubbard, A.M. Stockbridge, Mass.: Herman Willard, 1803.

Page 11. *The Jesuit Relations and Allied Comments: Travels and Explorations of the Jesuit Missionaries in North America (1610–1791),* edited by Edna Kenton. New York: Albert & Charles Boni, Inc., 1925.

Page 15. *The Early Jesuit Missions in North America,* translated by Rev. William Ingraham Kip, M.A. New York and London: Wiley & Putnam, 1846.

Page 19. *American Colonial Tracts Monthly, 1897–1898.* Vol. I, pp. 8–10.

Page 21. *Journal of Captain Robert Cholmley's Batman,* edited by Charles Hamilton. Norman, Okla.: University of Oklahoma Press, 1960.

Page 24. *Travels Through the Middle Settlements in North America in the Years 1759 and 1760,* by Andrew Burnaby. London, 1775.

Page 27. *Sketches of Eighteenth Century America,* by St. John de Crèvecoeur. New Haven: Yale University Press, 1925.

Page 30. *John Long's Voyages and Travels,* edited by Milo Quaife. Chicago: The Lakeside Press, R. R. Donnelley & Sons Co., 1922.

Pages 33 and 45. *George Washington, Writings,* edited by Jared Sparks. Boston, 1834. Vols. V and VII.

Page 36. *Letters and Memoirs Relating to the War of American Independence,* by Madame de Riedesel. Translated by William L. Stone. Albany: J. Munsell, 1867.

Page 40. *Our Revolutionary Forefathers: the Letters of François, Marquis de Barbé-Marbois.* New York: Duffield & Co., 1929.

Page 43. *Letters from America, 1776–1779,* translated by Ray W. Pettingill. Cambridge: The Riverside Press, Houghton Mifflin Co., 1924.

Page 48. *Correspondence of Charles, First Marquis Cornwallis.* London: John Murray, 1859.

Page 50. *The Revolutionary Journal of Baron Ludwig von Closen,* translated by Evelyn M. Acomb. Chapel Hill: University of North Carolina Press, 1958.

Page 51. *An Englishman in America: Being the Diary of Joseph Hadfield,* edited and annotated by Douglas S. Robertson. Toronto: The Hunter Rose Co., Ltd., 1933.

Page 57. *Journal of a Tour in Unsettled Parts of North America,* by Francis Baily, F.R.S. London: Bailey Brothers, 1856.

Page 60. *Retrospections of America,* by John Bernard. New York: Harper & Bros., 1887.

Page 62. *Jeffersonian America,* by Sir Augustus John Foster. San Marino, Calif.: Henry E. Huntington Library and Art Gallery, 1954.

Page 64. *Twenty-Four Letters from Labourers in America to their Friends in England,* edited by Benjamin Smith. London: Edward Rainford, 1829. Reprinted by the Sutro Branch, California State Library, 1939.

Pages 67 and 70. *Travels in the United States, 1827–1828,* by Basil Hall. Philadelphia: Carey, Lea & Carey, 1829.

Page 71. *Domestic Manners of the Americans,* by Mrs. Frances M. Trollope. London, 1832.

Page 75. *Journey to America,* by Alexis de Tocqueville. New Haven: Yale University Press, 1960.

Pages 79 and 82. *Society in America,* by Harriet Martineau. Paris: Beaudry's Europia Library, 1842.

Page 84. *American Notes,* by Charles Dickens. New York: Charles Scribner's Sons, 1843.

Page 86. *A Second Visit to the United States,* by Sir Charles Lyell. New York: Harper & Bros., 1849.

Page 88. *Louis Agassiz: His Life and Correspondence,* edited by Elizabeth Carey Agassiz. Boston: Houghton Mifflin Co., 1885.

Page 90. *Journal of Rudolph Friederich Kurz,* edited by J. N. B. Dewitt. Translated by Myrtis Jarrell. Washington, D.C.: Bureau of American Ethnology, The Smithsonian Institution, Bulletin 115.

Pages 95 and 99. *Homes of the New World,* by Fredrika Bremer. New York: Harper & Bros., 1853.

Page 102. *Three Years in California,* by J. D. Bothwick. Edinburgh and London: William Blackwood & Sons, 1858.

Page 105. *The Reminiscences of Carl Schurz.* New York: The McClure Co., 1907.

Page 111. *North America,* by Anthony Trollope. New York: Harper & Bros., 1862.

Page 114. *Six Months in the Federal States,* by Edward Dicey. London: Macmillan & Co., Ltd., 1863.

Page 116. *The Fremantle Diary,* by Lieutenant Colonel James Fremantle. Edited by Walter Lord. Boston: Little, Brown & Co., 1954.

Page 119. *A Visit to the Cities and Camps of the Confederate States,* by Fitzgerald Ross. Edinburgh and London: William Blackwood & Sons, 1865.

Page 121. *Four Years with the Army of the Potomac,* by Régis de Trobriand. Translated by George K. Dauchy. Boston: Ticknor & Co., 1889.

Page 125. *Last Winter in the United States,* by F. Barham Zincke. London: John Murray, 1868.

Page 133. *Offenbach in America: Notes of a Travelling Musician,* by Jacques Offenbach. New York: G. W. Carleton & Co., 1877.

Page 136. *Portrait of America: Letters of Henryk Sienkiewicz,* translated by Charles Morley. New York: Columbia University Press, 1959.

Page 138. *The Travels and Essays of Robert Louis Stevenson. The Amateur Emigrant.* New York: Charles Scribner's Sons, 1895.

Page 141. *Civilization in the United States,* by Matthew Arnold. Boston: Cupples & Hurd, 1888.

Page 144. *Critical Kit-Kats,* by Edmund Gosse. New York: Dodd, Mead & Co., 1896.

Page 148. *Life and Sport on the Pacific Slope,* by Horace Annesley Vachell. New York: Dodd, Mead & Co., 1900.

Page 151. *How the Other Half Lives,* by Jacob A. Riis. New York: Charles Scribner's Sons, 1890.

Pages 154 and 157. *From Sea to Sea,* by Rudyard Kipling. New York: Doubleday & McClure Co., 1899.

Page 160. *The Promised Land,* by Mary Antin. Boston and New York: Houghton Mifflin Co., 1912.